Living Conditions of URBAN SLUM CHILDREN IN TAMIL NADU

MJP PUBLISHERS

Living Conditions of URBAN SLUM CHILDREN IN TAMIL NADU

Dr. P. Satheswaran

&

Dr. M. Radhika

MJP PUBLISHERS

Chennai New Delhi

MJP PUBLISHERS

This edition has been published in India by arrangement with Carson Books, UK

ISBN 9789355289001

MJP Publishers
No. 44, Nallathambi Street,
Triplicane, Chennai 600 005

MJP 1732

Publisher : C. Janarthanan

Preface

Increasing urbanization is emerging as the most pervasive and dominant challenge as well as opportunity facing fast-growing country like India, today. Slum dwellers are highly vulnerable because of poor hygiene, over-crowding, lack of basic amenities such as water and sanitation, low availability and use of formal health services, particularly children. Urban slum children often live in extreme poverty, significantly impacting their access to education. Moreover, the opportunity cost of education for the poor families being low, motivating the families to send their children to primary schools and allowing them to continue the studies there until they finish their primary education are rather difficult. A poorer retention rate for the students belonging to these disadvantageous communities are largely explained by the socio-economic factors. Inadequate sanitation remains a leading cause of diarrheal disease and mortality among children in urban slums. The deprived physical environments present in slums are well-known to have adverse health effects on their residents. However, little is known about the health effects of the social environments in slums. Against this backdrop, the book has made an attempt to living conditions of urban slums children in Tamil Nadu with following specific objectives; to study the socio-economic status (SES) and living environment conditions of the respondents in urban slums, to analyses education attainment of children in schools in urban slums, and to find out the health status of children and performance of health care system in the study area.

The proposed study was conducted in the City of Salem, Tamil Nadu in India. It is the fifth largest city and a fast growing district in Tamil Nadu. The urban population is 13, 90, 000, which makes it the second largest city of Tamil Nadu in terms of population density. This district stands 4th place in case of slum population and 3rd in having the number of industries (Tamil Nadu: An Economic Appraisal, 2006-07 and 2007-08). Both primary, secondary and field based data have been used. The secondary data were collected from various reports at International, National, District level. For the collection of primary data, simple random sampling technique has been employed since the households are thickly spread in the slum region in a uniform size. A total of 400 households have been randomly selected for the study in the most densely populated slum regions of Salem Town. The data were analyzed by using appropriate statistical techniques including the test of significance. The book is presented in seven chapters. The first chapter views the definition of slum, growth of slums in global and national level, statement of the problem, objectives, methodology and limitations of the study. The second chapter deals with the theoretical background and review of literature relevant to the study. The third chapter highlights the overview of slum area. The fourth chapter analyses the enrolment the socio-economic status as well as living environment of the slum dwellers. The fifth chapter analyses the education attainment of children in schools in urban slums. The sixth chapter explains the health status of children and performance of health care system in the study area, and the final chapter deals major findings, conclusion and suggestion. The authors of this book have made genuine efforts to address the living conditions of urban slum children, with the aim of encouraging and motivating students and researchers to examine the dynamics of the challenges these children face in the context of modern economic development.

P. Satheswaran

M. Radhika

Contents

List of Tables

Chapter I

INTRODUCTION

1.1 INTRODUCTION

Increasing urbanization is emerging as the most pervasive and dominant challenge as well as opportunity facing India, today. Urban population in India has grown from 78.9 million in 1961 to 449 million in 2018 and is estimated to be double in next 25 years. Cities and towns are centres of agglomeration economies, investments, technology, innovation, economic growth and tertiary jobs. Their contribution to countries Gross Domestic Product (GDP) is immense. They are reservoirs of skills, capital and knowledge. They are the centres of innovation and creativity. They are the generators of resources for the national and state exchequers. They are also the hopes of millions of migrants from the rural hinterland and smaller settlements. With growth of the service sector and surge of the knowledge economy, the population pressure on cities is bound to escalate. They are increasingly face the negative consequences of rapid urbanization, such as polarization of population in large cities, high density, slums and squatter settlements, acute shortage of housing and basic civic amenities, degradation of environment, traffic congestion, pollution, poverty, unemployment, crime and social unrest.

An estimated 13.70 per cent of urban population (531 lakh in 2012) still subsists on incomes that are below the poverty line. Eighty percent of their meager earnings go towards food and energy, leaving very little for meeting the costs of living in an increasingly monetized society. The majority of them lives in slums and squatter settlements, in inhuman conditions that deny them dignity, shelter, security, and the right to basic civic amenities or social services, in an environment in which harbors crime, ill-health and disease, frequently raise demand on their resources that draws them deeper into vulnerability and poverty. Urbanization accompanied by sustained population growth due to large scale migration from rural areas to urban centres lead to mushrooming slum settlements in all cities and towns in India.

1.2 DEFINITION OF SLUM

Census of India (2011) defines slum areas as:

1. All specified areas in a town or city notified as 'Slum' by State, Local Government and Union Territory (UT) Administration under any Act including a 'Slum Act'.
2. All areas recognized as 'Slum' by State, Local Government and UT Administration, Housing and Slum Boards, which may have not been formally notified as slum under any act;
3. A compact area of at least 300 populations or about 60-70 households of poorly built congested tenements, in unhygienic environment usually with inadequate infrastructure and lacking in proper sanitary and drinking water facilities.

National Sample Survey Organization (NSSO) defines slum as a compact settlement with a collection of poorly built tenements, mostly of temporary nature, crowded together usually with inadequate sanitary and drinking water facilities in unhygienic conditions. Such an area was considered as a slum if at least 20 households lived in that area. Areas notified as slums by the respective municipalities, corporations, local bodies or development authorities were treated as "notified slums" and those unrecognized by the local bodies were considered to be "non-notified slums".

United Nation (UN) HABITAT defines "A slum is a contiguous settlement where the inhabitants are characterized as having inadequate housing and basic services. A slum is not often recognized and addressed by the public authorities as an integral or equal part of the city".

1.3 SLUM HOUSEHOLD

A slum household is defined as a group of individuals living under the same roof lacking one or more of the conditions below:

- Access to improved water
- Access to improved sanitation facilities
- Sufficient-living area not overcrowded

- Structural quality and durability of dwellings
- Security of tenure

1.4 CHARACTERISTICS OF SLUMS

A review of the definitions used by national and local governments, statistical offices, institutions involved in slum issues and public perceptions reveals the following attributes of slums.

1.4.1 LACK OF BASIC SERVICES

Lack of basic services is one of the most frequently mentioned characteristics of slum definitions worldwide. Lack of access to sanitation facilities and safe water sources is the most important feature, sometimes supplemented by absence of waste collection systems, electricity supply, surfaced roads and footpaths, street lighting and rainwater drainage. From safe drinking water to electricity, from basic health care to police services, from affordable public transport to fire and ambulance services, from sanitation sewer to paved roads, new slums usually lack all of these. Established, old slums sometimes garner official support and get some of these infrastructures such as paved roads and unreliable electricity or water supply (Chandrasekhar 2005).

1.4.2 SUBSTANDARD HOUSING OR ILLEGAL AND INADEQUATE BUILDING STRUCTURES

Many cities have building standards that set minimum requirements for residential buildings. Slum areas are associated with a high number of substandard housing structures; often the construction quality is inadequate to withstand heavy rains, high winds or other local climate and location. Paper, plastic, earthen floors, mud-and-wattle walls, wood held together by ropes, straw or torn metal pieces as roofs are some of the materials of construction. In some cases, brick and cement is used, but without attention to proper design and structural engineering requirements (Mandelker 1969). Various space and dwelling placement bylaws may also be extensively violated.

1.4.3 OVERCROWDING AND HIGH DENSITY

Overcrowding is associated with a low space per person, high occupancy rates, cohabitation by different families and a high number of single-room units. Many slum dwelling units are overcrowded, with five and more persons sharing a one-room unit used for cooking, sleeping and living. In a slum of Kolkata, India, over 10 people sometimes share a 45 m^2 room (Kundu 2003). In Kibera slum of Nairobi, Kenya, population density is estimated at 2,000 people per hectare or about 500,000 people in one square mile (UN-HABITAT 2008).

1.4.4 UNHEALTHY LIVING CONDITIONS & HAZARDOUS LOCATIONS

Unhealthy living conditions are the result of a lack of basic services, with visible, open sewers, lack of pathways, uncontrolled dumping of waste, polluted environments, etc. In cities, slums are located near lagoons, marshlands and rivers, they start at banks or on stilts above water or the dry river bed; in flat terrain, slums begin on lands unsuitable for agriculture, near city trash dumps, next to railway tracks and other shunned undesirable locations (Banerji 2009). Houses may be built on hazardous locations or land unsuitable for settlement, such as floodplains, in proximity to industrial plants with toxic emissions or waste disposal sites and on areas subject to landslip. The layout of the settlement may be hazardous because of a lack of access ways and high densities of dilapidated structures. Some slums risk man-made hazards such as toxic industries, traffic congestion and collapsing infrastructures (Davis 2006).

1.4.5 INSECURE TENURE AND IRREGULAR OR INFORMAL SETTLEMENTS

A number of definitions consider lack of security of tenure as a central characteristic of slums, and regard lack of any formal document entitling the occupant to occupy the land or structure as prima facie evidence of illegality and slum occupation. Informal or unplanned settlements are often regarded as synonymous with slums. Many definitions emphasize both informality of occupation and the noncompliance of settlements with land-use plans. The main factors contributing to non-compliance are settlements built on land reserved for non-residential purposes, or which are invasions of non-urban land. In the sphere, 51 percent of slums are based on invasion to private land in Sub-Saharan Africa, 39 percent in North Africa and West Asia, 10 percent in South Asia, 40 percent in East Asia, and 40 percent in Latin America and the Caribbean (Flood 2006).

1.4.6 POVERTY AND SOCIAL EXCLUSION

Income or capability poverty is considered, with some exceptions, as a central characteristic of slum areas. It is not seen as an inherent characteristic of slums, but as a cause and consequence of slum conditions. Slum conditions are physical and statutory manifestations that create barriers to human and social development. Furthermore, slums are areas of social exclusion that are often perceived to have high levels of crime and other measures of social dislocation. In some definitions, such areas are associated with certain vulnerable groups of population, such as recent immigrants, internally displaced persons or ethnic minorities.

1.4.7 MINIMUM SETTLEMENT SIZE

Many slum definitions also require some minimum settlement size for an area to be considered a slum, so that the slum constitutes a distinct precinct and is not a single dwelling. The Indian census definition, states that at least 300 people or 60 households living in a settlement cluster.

1.5 URBANIZATION AND SLUM

With Industrial revolution rural folk started migrating in small numbers to cities where the new industries were located. In places outside Europe, the same phenomenon was repeated nearly 100 years ago. Till then, the world's urban centres had barely five per cent of the total population. Towards the end of 2007, the world has reached yet another milestone where the urban population and rural population of the world are equal to each other. This has brought new economic opportunities and advantages to people who have migrated to cities and towns. But this has also created the phenomenal growth of slums all over the world. According to demographers, nearly all population growth between 2000 and 2030 is expected in urban areas of the developing world. The U.N. Habitat's Publication State of the World's Cities 2006-2007 says one in every three urbanites lives in slums (The Hindu, 2009).

As per Census of India 2011, out of 4,041 Statutory Towns in India, 2543 towns are reported as slum towns (63 percent). About 1.08 lakhs are Total Slum Enumeration Blocks (SEBs) in the country, in that Maharashtra (21,359) reported as the largest number of Slum Enumeration Blocks. Maharashtra offers opportunities for many migrants. Most of the slum dwellers are not necessarily Maharastrians; over a few generations they may be absorbed. The total number of urban households is 789 lakhs. About one sixth of urban households are reported as slum households. 38 percent of the slum households are in 46 Million Plus Cities and remaining 61.9 percent resides in other cities. Andhra Pradesh (35.7 percent), Chhattisgarh (31.9 percent), Madhya Pradesh (28.3 percent), Odisha (23.1 percent) and West Bengal (21.9 percent) are the top five states, where the proportion of slum households to urban households is higher. In million plus cities, the proportion of slum households to urban households with high proportion is in Greater Visakhapatnam (44.1 percent), Jabalpur Cantt (43.3 percent), Greater Mumbai (41.3 percent), Vijayawada (40.6 percent) and Meerut (40 percent).

1.6 HEALTH CONDITIONS IN SLUMS

Slums are considered a major public health concern and potential breeding grounds of drug resistant diseases for the entire city, the nation, as well as the global community (Alirol 2011). Poor housing conditions can be deadly for those suffering from a disease which destroys the victim's immune system. Overcrowding leads to faster and wider spread of diseases due to the limited space in slum housing. Furthermore, diseases can sometimes lead to high mortality in slums. Inadequate health services engender a higher rate of disease transmission in slums than that in non-slum areas. Slum dwellers usually experience a high rate of disease. Diseases reported in slums include cholera, measles, malaria, dengue, typhoid, drug resistant tuberculosis, and other epidemics. Children's health in slums address that cholera and diarrhea are especially common among young children. Poor water quality, a manifest example, is a cause of many major illnesses including malaria, diarrhea and trachoma (WHO 2004).

Child malnutrition is more common in slums than in non-slum areas. In Mumbai and New Delhi, 47 percent and 51 percent of slum children under the age of five are stunted and 35 percent and 36 percent of them are underweighted. These children all suffered from third-degree malnutrition, the most severe level, according to WHO standards. Dr. Abhay Bang's report shows that malnutrition kills 56,000 children annually in urban slums in India (The Times of India 2011).

Health is a major economic issue for slum residents. The unhealthy physical environment leads to sickness, which leads to costs for continuing medical treatment, which leads to reduction of workdays and economic loss.

Economic loss leads to inability to invest in clean environment. Measures of human capability poverty include health as a prime component because, without good health, the chances of leaving behind poverty and the slums are negligible. Poor health, along with loss of wage employment, is the major shock dimension of urban poverty, while chronic ill health is a major determinant of chronic poverty. Urban workers, reliant on wage labour, are particularly dependent on ongoing good health. The inability of a principal wage earner to continue working, accompanied by the subsequent debt to meet medical costs, is enough to throw lower income families into poverty for extended periods.

1.7 EDUCATION IN SLUMS

Literacy is seen as a pre-requisite for economic growth, social mobility and political stability. Illiteracy, by contrast has frequently been related to increased poverty, under development, political volatility and economic stagnation (Roberts 2000). Increased urbanisation adversely affects the quality of life of the people some times and many times it leads to negligence of education for economically deprived section of the society especially in the slums and squatter settlement. However, the way literacy gets defined the fact remains that because of historical, social and economic reasons different regions not only have different level of literacy, but there may be disparate levels of literacy attainment between various social groups, locations and gender within a region. In general, the level of literacy in slums area has been found less than the non-slum areas in India.

The overall picture of education in India implies that educational opportunity and attainment for the urban deprived are much lower than for the affluent section of the population. Successive policy document on education have made no mention of the problems of education among the urban disadvantaged. Consequently, there is no coherent perspective on tacking her problems of education of such children and not is there adequate information on the educational provision reaching disadvantage children in urban areas (Govinda 2002).

Poverty or low income, adversely affect the quality and quantity of education at the macro country level (UN Millennium Project 2005) the mesa region and school levels (GOI, 2002) and the micro household level (Haper et al 2003). Moreover, much education research shows that education deprivation is caused not merely by poverty but also by related factors (Dyer and Rose 2006). In the case of India these factors might be closely related to gender, caste, labour market opportunity, the quality learning and facility in school.

1.8 ENVIRONMENT IN SLUMS

The environment in Indian slums is abominable and malodorous. As the slums get crowded, the environment gets overpopulated and as a result, there is twice as much trash, corpses and human excretion. The physical environment of the slums depends on the outcome of facilities of habitation, available water, toilets, drainage, and lighting. Unfortunately, high levels of pollution, lack of basic needs, and room-crowding are some of the basic characteristics of slum housing. The roads in the Indian slums are heavily polluted and the shacks are lined up so tight that the residents have to walk in single-file past the sewers. Real toilets, sinks, and showers are not available to the slum-dwellers so they do their personal needs any place that is available. The children in the Indian slum community are being affected by the current living environment. The surrounding environment affects children due to the diverse types of animals also living in the slums (Sathya Sai Baba 2001).

1.9 STATEMENT OF THE PROBLEM

One consequence of rapid pace of urbanisation is the incapacity of developing countries to provide them basic necessities like shelter, water, sanitation, health and education for slums dwellers. Growth of slums in Indian cities seems phenomenal and slum population in India constituted 17.5 per cent of urban population in 1981 which rose up to 21.5 per cent in 1991 and the census of 2011 also shows an increasing trend. Though Tamil Nadu has been acclaimed as a Medium Human Development Indicator state (Tamil Nadu Human Development Report, 2015) in India, the working and living environment of the urban slum is extremely worse and it created a detrimental effect on their health and health status.

Urban poor are largely understood as people living in overcrowded and dilapidated slums or in squatters built on pavements, along railway tracks, besides pipelines, under bridges, on ill-drained marshlands and any vacant land available to them, in the urban areas. Human living conditions in the absence of basic civic amenities such as safe and adequate water supply, sewerage and sanitation and toilets, has been precarious and miserable for the health, safety and comfort in such communities. Due to their unhealthy site location and living and working in pollution-prone environment, it is easily perceived that it is the urban poor who are bearing the brunt of increasing urban environmental problems.

Urban poverty, ill health, and living in slums are intrinsically interwoven. Poverty is the root cause of ill health in the sprawling slums. Urban poverty has many facets that need to be considered such as housing as well as levels of income and consumption. Poverty is conventionally defined in terms of incomes that are inadequate to permit the purchase of necessities, including food and safe water in sufficient quantity. Food security is a critical health issue for the urban poor most households are food-insecure.

Proximate causes of ill health in urban slums are lack of adequate basic services (clean toilets, bathing units, garbage disposal, drinking water), inadequate food intake and low levels of nutrition - weakens the immune system there by making the body prone to infections, lack of financial resources - to ensure sustained medical attention for various diseases, mistreatment and bad behaviour at government hospitals compel the poor to avail of private alternatives and lack of information about proper state owned and managed medical benefits.

Slum dwellers are highly vulnerable because of poor hygiene, overcrowding, lack of basic amenities such as water and sanitation, low availability and use of formal health services. Inadequate sanitation remains a leading cause of diarrheal disease and mortality among children in urban slums. An open sewer runs through the centre of few slums. When it rains, the sewage overflows, making its way into people's homes. The open–air waste attracts rats and is a breeding ground for pestilence and disease. Some of the waste dumped around proved extremely toxic and hazardous, which through their indiscriminate dumping have brought about the death of livestock, environmental pollutions and an increasing number of incidents that have caused ill-health and epidemic of diseases which in some cases have led to lost of human lives. Additionally, urban air quality is polluted from industry and vehicles and indoor air can be especially toxic from fumes of indoor cooking stoves. Children are especially susceptible to lung disease from air pollution.

The deprived physical environments present in slums are well-known to have adverse health effects on their residents. However, little is known about the health effects of the social environments in slums. Though there are studies, which present slum housing problem, environmental conditions, slum upgrading and related policy analysis. There is dearth of studies seeking to correlate the degree of health injuries caused by poor human living environment in urban slum communities.

Moreover, there are still atleast one lakh habitations in the country having no schooling facility within one kilometer. Coupled with it, there are various systemic issues related to inadequate school infrastructure, poorly functioning schools, high teacher absenteeism, large number of vacancies in teaching posts and poor quality of teaching. The Sarva Shiksha Abigyan (SSA) seeks to provide quality elementary education. The basic problem with widening the coverage of elementary education in India is that, there are a large number of students from challenging backgrounds both in rural and urban areas. As the private returns from elementary education are low, the parents of the students belonging to the disadvantaged families do not assign much value to elementary education. Moreover, the opportunity cost of education for the poor families being low, motivating the families to send their children to primary schools and allowing them to continue the studies there until they finish their primary education are rather difficult. A poorer retention rate for the students belonging to these disadvantageous communities are largely explained by the socio-economic factors.

The incidence of absence due to sickness is quite high in the schools in this locality. Migration is another factor that hampers the schooling of the children of the poor families. The parents of the children who are engaged in petty jobs in different factories have no job security. Periodic job loss is a common phenomenon here. As the family fails to get an alternative means of livelihood in the locality, they move to some other locality, not necessarily near the school where the child has been enrolled. The casualty is the schooling of the child. Lack of school environment (infrastructure that is drinking water facilities, separate toilet for girls and boys, play ground, number of class rooms, etc.), curricula and security also plays a pivotal role in the enrolment of students. Hence, this study is going to examine the enrollment and retention of children in schools and to find out the reasons for poor attendance behaviour of both teachers and students in urban slum.

In addition to health and education, urban slums stem from the lack of access to and more demand for basic amenities. Basic service provisions are either absent or inadequate in slums. Lack of drinking water, clean and sanitary environment, adequate housing, garbage disposal and sewage threats to the health of slum dwellers, particularly for women and children because, they spend most of their time in and around the unhygienic environment. The demand for basic services is lacking, because there is no agency or institution (state or central) that is willing to assess the needs and fulfill the demand. Supply side techniques alone cannot solve infrastructure problem and public sector agencies and the community participation also need to become more responsive to societal needs. Inability to basic service results form a service of manmade institutional bottlenecks that prevent the poor from accessing services created primarily in their name. Hence an integrated approach among health, education and living environment will be attempted in this research study.

1.10 OBJECTIVES

Keeping this research problem the following objectives are framed

- To study the socio-economic status (SES) and living environment conditions of the respondents in urban slums.
- To analyses education attainment of children in schools in urban slums.
- To find out the health status of children and performance of health care system in the study area.

1.11 FORMULATION OF HYPOTHESIS

Based on the research problem and objectives of the study, it is hypothesized that

- There is association between child education and socio-economic conditions of slum children in Salem District.
- There is association between type of disease and living environment index of slum children.
- There is no significant difference between the health problem and socio-economic conditions of slum children.

1.12 METHODOLOGY FRAMEWORK

1.12.1 SOURCE OF DATA COLLECTION

The present study has been carried out with both primary and secondary data. The secondary data was obtained from the Census Reports of

Government of India, District Statistical Handbook of Statistics, Report of the Committee on Slum Statistics, and various Government reports published by Bureau of Economics and Statistics, Government of Tamilnadu. In order to collect the primary data a structured and pre-tested questionnaire has been designed in such a way that it satisfies the primary objectives of the study.

1.12.2 SAMPLING TECHNIQUE

For the collection of primary data, simple random sampling technique has been employed since the households are thickly spread in the slum region in a uniform size. A total of 400 households have been randomly selected for the study in the most densely populated slum regions of Salem Town. There are 111 notified slum areas in Salem district consisting of four zones i.e. Suramangalam zone, Hasthampatti zone, Ammapet zone and Kondalampatty zone. The total number of slum households were 39022 which constitute the total slum population of 2,45,926 in Salem district. From each zone 1 per cent of the households were selected as sample respondents.

1.12.3 AREA OF THE STUDY

The research is conducted in the City of Salem, Tamil Nadu in India. It is the fifth largest city and a fast growing district in Tamil Nadu. The urban population is 13, 90, 000, which makes it the second largest city of Tamil Nadu in terms of population density. This district stands 4th place in case of slum population and 3rd in having the number of industries (Tamil Nadu: An Economic Appraisal, 2006-07 and 2007-08). Similarly this district falls under the category of medium Human Development Index (HDI) with respect to health and education (Tamil Nadu Human Development Report, 2017). For the purpose of study the slum areas has been selected based on different income levels and cultural groups, commercially developed area with good transport links, the proximity to labour market, most hazardous slum, and industrialized areas.

1.12.4 TOOLS APPLIED

For the data analysis the appropriate statistical tools like mean, percent, Chi-square test, Likert scaling technique and ANOVA were used. Econometric tools like Ordinary Least Square Regression were employed.

1.13 LIMITATION OF THE STUDY

It should be noted that the slums surveyed are limited to notified slums. Because of this, the sample is unlikely to include the poorest of the poor, such as the homeless, the destitute and short-term seasonal or new migrants. It is also worth mentioning that only those who remain in the slums are covered in the survey, while some households might have moved out of the slums to better residential areas or returned to their place of origin. This is particularly relevant for non-migrants and long-term migrants.

1.14 CHAPTERIZATION

This research work is divided into five chapters

- The first chapter views the definition of slum, growth of slums in global and national level, statement of the problem, objectives, methodology and limitations of the study.
- The second chapter deals with the theoretical background and review of literature relevant to the study.
- The third chapter highlights the overview of slum area.
- The fourth chapter analyses the enrolment the socio-economic status as well as living environment of the slum dwellers.
- The fifth chapter analyses the education attainment of children in schools in urban slums.
- The sixth chapter explains the health status of children and performance of health care system in the study area.
- The final chapter deals major findings, conclusion and suggestion.

Chapter II

THEORETICAL AND EMPIRICAL EVIDENCES

2.1 INTRODUCTION

The present chapter is divided into two sections. In Section I, the researcher discusses the theoretical frame and in Section II, the empirical studies carried out by various researchers are discussed for operational purpose.

2.2 THEORETICAL EVIDENCE

The health capital approach appears to be a very useful framework, since it offers a system that can accommodate most variables of interest for the purpose of this study. Since health production models do not provide any in-depth view of health knowledge. This offers fresh ideas to economic approaches. Some of which are directly applicable to the human capital tradition of modeling health and knowledge.

Economic models that are most relevant and commonly used in the analysis of prevention and health promotion are human capital theory and expected utility theory (Kenkel, 2000). The basic difference between these two theoretical foundations is the emphasis they place on uncertainty as an element of consumer behaviour. In the centre of the human capital approach there is household production theory, and initially the health related models were not much concerned with uncertainty. In the more recent work models have been modified the other hand, builds on the consumers response to uncertainty and has been successfully applied in the analysis of insurance behaviour. These two approaches and try to point out their main advantages and disadvantages for modeling health promotion.

2.2.1 THE HUMAN CAPITAL APPROACH

The Theory of the Allocation of Time, (Becker, 1965) outlined a model where households are seen as producers of "commodities" instead of solely consumers of goods and services. Households are assumed to derive utility from the basic commodities they produce by combining their own time with market goods. Hence, the utility associated with a market good is conditional on the time that is allocated to its consumption. This gives rise to more restricted utility maximization, since in addition to the traditional money budget constraint the time budget must also be accounted for, as well as appropriate production technologies (Becker, 1965).

Grossman (1972b,a) used the household production framework to develop his model of the demand for health. He defined health as a durable capital stock, and hence implied that the end product is not health as such but the services this capital good yields (Becker, 1965; Grossman, 1972 b, a). In Grossman's formulation, individuals derive utility from the services that health capital yields and from the consumption of other commodities. The stock of health capital depreciates over time and the consumer can produce gross investments in it according to a household production function using medical care and their own time as inputs. It is assumed that the efficiency of the production process depends on individual's stocks of other forms of human capital, especially education.

In Grossman's model the time span for inter-temporal optimization is determined endogenously by defining a minimum level of health (deal stock) below which death follows. The yield from the individual's stock of health capital is defined as the total number of healthy days in each year, which generates utility directly, since being healthy yields utility ("Consumption" motives), and indirectly, since being healthy yields income which in turn can be used to purchase goods or to produce commodities which influence utility ("investment" motives).

In the Grossman model, as in household production models in general, the demand for the medical care, and other market goods, is indirectly derived from the demand for the commodities that households choose to produce. The optimal level of health capital for any individual is determined by the point at which the marginal cost of investment in health capital is equal to the marginal utility of healthy days (Grossman, 1972b).

Muurinen (1982a) developed Grossman's model to produce more general results, especially regarding the role of education and effects the life-style and environmental factors. Muurinen (1982a) criticizes Grossman's model as being too unspecific about the role of education and she suggests that education has an effect on the rate at which health stock is used up (depreciates) in order to produce services, and hence links the allocative efficiency gains of education to the concept of use-related depreciation of health stock. She claims that this approach provides useful device for including the effects of behavioural, life style and environmental factors in the model, without being limited by the positive gross investment assumption used by Grossman (Muurinen, 1982a).

Muurinen (1982a) adopts a more general concept of health outcome, by viewing productive benefits generated by the stock of the health as increased capacity to perform tasks either at home or in the labour force and allowing the value of that improvement to depend on the individual's circumstances. She abandons the framework of household production by assuming that the use of medical care requires a fixed amount of time, i.e. that time does not have a distinct role as an input. In her model, healthy time, as a proxy for the benefits produced by health capital, does not have any inherent theoretical significance, and hence can be replaced or ignored if necessary (Muurinen, 1982a).

Cropper (1977) introduced a couple of modifications to Grossman's model, which are particularly interesting from the point of view of health promotion. She based her developments on the pure consumption version of Grossman's formulation by assuming that investment in health is driven by the desire to avoid disutility related to illness as such, rather than monetary losses due to sick time (Cropper, 1977). She distinguishes between illness and death as, respectively, temporary and permanent interruptions to the individual's utility stream. She allows for uncertainty in the relationship between the stock of health capital and the service flow the stock by assuming that the critical level of stock below which illness occurs is a random variable. In other words, even at a high level of health capital an individual cannot be sure that illness is avoided. Cropper designs the model specifically to analyse minor illnesses and assumes that short-lasting conditions do not affect the level of health stock. She assumes that individual's use of medical care is related to a random event of failing ill and that preventive health services alone can be treated as genunine investment in health capital. This distinction between the roles of preventive and curative care is very important for the analysis of health promotion.

Using this framework, Cropper also models the decision to choose an occupation where an individual is exposed to industrial pollutant but is also paid a higher wage. She finds that if the pollutant does not yield immediate disutility and if the worker ever accepts to work in a risky occupation, it may be optimal for him always to expose himself to some amount of pollution. The implication of this is that, even after discovering the potential health risk, a worker may make a rational choice not to quit such an occupation (Cropper, 1977). This result follows from the assumption that he is currently alive as a basis for the decision on whether or not to further expose himself to the pollutant. This is another important result of Cropper's model which can be applied to the context of health promotion, in particular to the modeling of individual's response to the information on risks of smoking and excessive alcohol use.

It is acknowledged that the Grossman type of deterministic health capital model have been criticized on the basis that it neglects the influence of uncertainty. For instance, Zwelfel and Breyer (1997) point out that ignoring the possibility of stochastic shocks, such as accidents or major illnesses which may result in large and permanent decreases in the level of health capital leads to overestimates of an individual's control of his own health in the long run. These shocks may limit individual's choice of the means for any further health improvements or even dramatically reduce the length of the whole planning horizon (Zwifel and Breyer, 1997). Considering these possibilities in theoretical modeling it is possible to study our framed research problem and objective under the health capital approach.

2.2.2 HOUSEHOLDS AND UTILISATION OF HEALTH CARE

Studies of utilisation of health care generally use the individual as the unit of analysis. Much of this work has taken its point of departure in Grossman's seminal work (1972), where he argued that the individual produces the commodity"good health". This commodity is part of the individual's human capital and affects the total amount of time the individual can spend on productive activities. Even if Grossman's work provided the field of health economics with great input, it lacked the fact that individuals are household members and take much influence from (willing or not willingly) from other household members. Much speaks for using the household as the unit of analysis (some individuals do of course live in single person households).

Income and education is among the most influential factors for health care utilization (Grossman, 1972a, 1972b). However, other factors such as age also influence utilisation since age reflects on perceived benefit and income. There have been a number of studies showing relationship between household income and utilisation of health care (Grossman, 1972; Muurinen, 1982; Wagstaff; 1986, 1993, Bolin et al, 1999). However all these have shown a relatively weak relationship, while studies on developing countries shown that the income elasticity is rather high. Utilisation of health care is in practice very much influenced by decisions by the provider, physicians advice etc. However, the first contact with the health system is taken by the individual and expected access cost is probably the largest determinant of seeking care. Access cost is a combination of several factors such as, distance to health facilities, waiting time at the facility, out of pocket payments etc, i.e. monetary costs as well as time costs (Le Grand, 1982). Time costs include time for reaching the facility, waiting time and time for consultation. Monetary costs include fees for services and travelling costs. Costs of access are usually an important explanatory factor of differences in health care utilisation between different social groups in developing countries (Gertler and van der Gaag, 1990, Timyan et al, 1993). Studies on developed countries commonly focus on annual income as a proxy for a household's economic situation. However, household *consumption* could be a betterapproximation of economic circumstances, including a household's long term and short-term ability to pay for health care (Steen Carlsson and Lyttkens, 1997). This fact is even more important to consider in a developing country context where annual income often is an inappropriate measure of economic circumstances due to e.g. subsistence farming. Behrman and Deolalikar (1988) also find household consumption to be the natural approximation of the household's economic circumstances in their analysis of decisions, which act as proximate determinants of individual health status. Jacobson (1998) extends Grossman's model into a model in which the family is viewed as the producer of health. In this model, the family have common preferences and her main conclusion is that not only the individual's own income, but the family's combined resources are used in the production of health.

2.3 REVIEW OF LITERATURE

Review of literature helps in bridging the gap between the present and past researches. This allows the researcher to find the unexplored areas and dimensions in particular field. This provides a critical insight into the forms and methods used by different persons and help to divert the researcher to form a new way for the analysis. The present chapter concentrates on views and findings of different researchers related to socio-economic conditions, living environment, health status and education of children in urban slums. In the present study, the reviews are categorized into four aspects viz.,

- Studies related to general issues
- Living environment related studies
- Reviews on education of slum children
- Health related studies and others

2.3.1 STUDIES RELATED TO GENERAL ISSUES

As the present study focuses on slums, the literature related to general issues were likely relevant to socio-economic conditions of slum dwellers, urbanization, slum housing and development schemes, type and magnitude of slum population in India. Details of few reviews dealing with these issues are given below.

Geetha and Madhura Swaminathan (1996) presented the socioeconomic characteristics of households in the slum settlement and attempted to identify the prevalence of undernutrition among children using the available anthropometric data. The basic amenities in the area, however, were pitifully inadequate in the slum communities of Mumbai. The slum was populated mainly by people from Maharashtra, Uttar Pradesh and Tamil Nadu. The monthly income of households in the sample averaged Rs. 1,954 and over one-third of all households had a low per capita income, of less than Rs 300 per month. Information on physical assets indicated that most households possessed a limited number of assets. Male workers in the surveyed households were predominantly general production-related workers whereas female workers were engaged mainly in low-income service occupations. Anthropometric indicators revealed that a high proportion of children in the sample, particularly girls, were undernourished Systematic public action is required to improve the nutritional status of children in this settlement as in other urban slums.

Naveen Kumar and Suresh Chand Aggarwal (2003) aimed to determine the extent of poverty in Delhi slums through consumption patterns, employment and educational status of the slum population. The study brings out significant social and economic aspects of the people living in Delhi's slums, including low level of education of the migrants, gender disparity in economic status, and significant number of households below the poverty line. The results emphasised the need for a positive employment generation policy among urban slum dwellers. There is also a need to generate employment and provide facilities at the origin of migration in order to check the influx into Delhi.

Nihar Ranjan Rout (2008) attempted to understand the process of slum growth in the city of Bhubaneswar and to find out the growth of slum population in the city and to know about the reasons behind migratory movements to the urban slums and to get an idea about the living conditions and problems faced by the slum dwellers. Landlessness was found to be the major reason behind migratory movements to the slums, followed by economic problem, irregular work and unemployment at their place of origin. Apart from poor living conditions and health related problems, slum dwellers also reported about the problems of poor civic facilities, fear of displacement, irregular work, and insufficient income. According to their perceptions, major problems were related to housing, employment and environment, compared to those related to society and social life. Slums are not problems that have to be solved; rather they represent a solution of shelter for the poor. Now the challenge for the policy makers was to facilitate the types of movement that were most likely to lead to alleviation of poverty, while protecting the slum dwellers from abuse and exploitation.

Sean Fox (2008) informed that three historically contingent factors were found to have a significant influence on contemporary slum incidence that is rapid urban growth, colonial legacies of governance and political fractionalisation. In a second stage of analyzed an instrumental variables strategy indicated that slum incidence exerts a negative effect on income. This relationship might reflect un-captured agglomeration benefits due to poor urban governance and management in the face of rapid urban growth and the possibility that slum incidence is a proxy for quality of governance more generally.

Alamgir, Jabbar and Islam (2009) attempted to determine the factors affecting the livelihood of the socioeconomic improvement of migrants and to analyze the causes of rural-urban migration in slum areas. Slum areas have no available formal education facilities and slum people were found to be engaged in rickshaw pulling, day labourer, petty business, small job services etc. This paper analysed that migration and taking in micro credit were beneficial for the slum dwellers. Receiving and utilizing micro credit income level, consumption, expenditure and socio-economic status of the slum dwellers improved to some extent. Due to participation of slum dwellers in Non Government Organisations (NGOs), their economic, social and decision making improved substantially. Credit disbursement through NGOs with integrated approach could bring positive changes in the life of poor slum women as well as their community. Findings showed that fifty six per cent people migrated to Dhaka city for economic reason. Factors of migration had a significant contribution of rural urban migration and also significant livelihood improvement has taken place due to micro credit. At the individual level, the women were benefited in terms of mobility and skill, self confidence, widening of interests, access to financial services, build own savings, competence in public affairs and status at home and in the community that lead a better awareness for enhancing women's empowerment. However, there is a need for proper training for sustainable result in the long run.

Rajnish Kumar et al (2009) attempted to revisit the caste issue in the Indian context, analysed a sample of households from the slums of four cities. Vulnerability conceptualised in terms of several socio-economic and demographic indicators exists among most of the social categories though the relative size of deprivation varies across social groups. In a binomial logit framework, based on the pooled sample, the extent of decline in the probability of experiencing well-being beyond a threshold limit is sharper for the socially backward classes than the others. However, in individual cities such a pattern is not so conspicuous implying that all the social categories are equally vulnerable. These findings have important policy implications, indicating that policy initiatives for deprived areas irrespective of caste factor are more important than the caste-based support measures. Developmental expenditure and employment programmes are some of the important dimensions of government initiatives to reduce urban poverty.

Ben Arimah (2010) accounted for differences in the prevalence of slums among African countries. One of the most enduring physical manifestations of social exclusion in African cities is the proliferation of slums and informal settlements. People living in these settlements experience the most deplorable living and environmental conditions. They are also excluded from participating in the economic social, political and cultural spheres of the city. The empirical analyzed identified substantial inter-country variations in the incidence of slums; and indicates that higher levels of income, greater financial stability and investment in infrastructure will reduce the incidence of slums and by extension- reduce social exclusion. Conversely, the external debt burden, high levels of inequality, unplanned and unmanaged urban growth, and the exclusionary nature of the regulatory framework governing the provision of planned residential land contribute to the prevalence of slums and squatter settlements- thus increasing levels of social exclusion.

Uddin Haider (2010) examined the rural-urban migration patterns of poor migrants who move to Rajshahi city, Bangladesh, either on their own or with their families. It explored the consequences that the migration process driven by economic and social reasons has on unemployment and due to poverty. The findings of this work show that the factors and impact of migration on their livelihood. It was also finding out the fulfilment status about their dreams which they were shown before migration. The underlying efforts to improve economic status in urban Bangladesh, thus, is that of urban poor, particularly the urban migrants, who are growing more rapidly than the rural poor due to heavy rural-urban migration. Urban planners should be concerned about the rapidly expanding cities and the concentration of perhaps disaffected migrants in urban areas. The study results highlight the need to target migrant groups and urban poor within urban areas in the provision of availability of work care services.

Wendy Olsen (2010) used evidence from 91 individuals in 58 households out of a sample of 800 in five of the 1230 slums of Chennai, Tamil Nadu. It finds both a considerable diversity of economic circumstances and of economic experiences during the growth slow-down, price rises, heat and floods of 2008-09. Qualitative Comparative Analysis (QCA) is used to compare the experience of households with that of a matched sample of individuals. It revealed the different characteristics of individual- from household experiences. Older individuals suffered more. Individual households had higher than average consumer to worker ratios experienced downward change. The majority of households which experienced 'downward' changes were concentrated in the wage-work group, implying that the remaining households that were self-employed or had small businesses were better protected from the combined economic and environmental insults. Households depending upon trading and retail income were more protected from the economic and environmental insults than those in 'services' and manufacturing sectors. The data also showed interesting patterns of, to which they kept contributing during this period and patterns of debt that were comparatively high in relation to income.

Sohail Ahmad and Mack Joong Choi (2011) reviewed the rapid urbanization and proliferation of uncontrolled settlements in Delhi and shed some light on the characteristics of households and housings there. The data used included a survey of approximately 225 households, interviewed with various stakeholders and official census data. The analysis revealed wide variations in socioeconomic and dwelling-unit characteristics among different types of settlements. The results showed a lack of physical and social infrastructure across the settlements. The households in the slum settlement had a very low income level, while households in the unauthorized colony and urban village had relatively high amounts of income. Urban infrastructure provisions were identified as a key area for planning intervention in order to integrate these settlements into sustainable residential developments. Besides such provisions, economic interventions were also necessary for slum households.

Amitabh Kundu (2013) pointed out that the Rajiv Awas Yojana Schemes (RAYs) in operation lack a reliable framework for identifying non-tenable slums and legitimate slum households that are entitled to get dwelling units. Speedy implementation of the programme on a national scale is needed to cover the total slum population in a time-bound manner, without which the mission would be an empty dream. The RAY is a well-intentioned programme but unlike the (Mahatma Gandhi National Rural Government Organisations) MGNREGS it has no formal constitutional guarantee. The surveys conducted in the first three years of its existence by the ministry concerned lack a macro perspective and have not been able to resolve local-level issues to do with implementation. The absence of a road map for implementing the mission in a time-bound manner in the whole country or even in a selected set of cities has resulted in a lot of uncertainty.

Sufaira (2013) analysed the socio-economic conditions of the slum dwellers in Kannur District. The researcher employed Chi-square test in order to find out the relationship between living environment and health status. The result shown that living environment adversely affects the health status of the people. Morbidity rate is slightly higher in non-notified area than notified area. The study showed that in the notified area conditions of slum dwellers are better than that of non-notified area. In the non- notified area health and living conditions are continuous to be very poor and disgusting. In short multi-prolonged strategy required not only to address the needs of slum dwellers for shelter but also the problems of urban poverty, unemployment, low incomes and lack of access to basic urban services.

Upinder Sawhney (2013) aimed to analyses certain demographic attributes of the slum population in India, the public policy response towards the same. It also reviewed certain programmes designed by the government to control the growth of slums and the efforts to rehabilitate the slum-dwellers. It concludes that the policy of urban development must focus on slum clearance and rehabilitation of the poor and public-private partnership mode is a way out for integrated urban development. To create 'inclusive cities' in future there is an urgent need for improving the local government capacity to meet these challenges and ensure that the allocated funds reach the target population. There is a dire necessity for 'good governance' at all levels of the government. The ideal situation can be reached if institutional framework for appointing a regulator for urban development can be worked out.

2.3.2 LIVING ENVIRONMENT RELATED STUDIES

Studies in this section trace the living conditions, absence of basic amenities such as drinking water, sanitation, electricity, garbage disposal and its consequences on slum dwellers. Several studies have been carried out to look at this aspect. Below few selected studies are briefly discussed.

Prasada Rao (1972) conducted a study to find out the influence of socio-economic, housing and environmental factors on the morbidity of children in 3 slum communities, viz., Debraipet, Keerapalayam and Vanarapet, near Pondicherry. 399 households were studied. The total population was 2188 with an average family size of 6. Pre-school children constituted 25.3 per cent. The average income per family per month was 97.30 rupees which is much lower than the national figure. The majority of the families were self-employed either professionally or otherwise and their livelihood depended on the availability of the work. Faulty feeding of children was seen in 80 per cent of the families. Bad housing, unsatisfactory environmental sanitation, poverty, illiteracy and ignorance of the parents made the children fall prey to diseases like respiratory infections, gastro-intestinal disorders, skin diseases, worm infestations and malnutrition. Home visits by the social workers and the public health nurse to educate and demonstrate both young and old womenfolk, the right type of diet to be given to children at the right time and to inculcate in them a sense of personal hygiene is very much needed.

Rashda Azhar, Sycda Khizra Aslam and Muhammad Akhtar (1992) highlighted the living conditions of rural migrants in slum dwellings of Faisalabad city. The sample consisted of 600 respondents. Inadequate drinking water facilities, Lack of proper disposal of garbage facilities, lack of lavotorics and no proper drainage system tended to create a serious problem of sanitation. It gives a bleak picture of the standard of life of the poor slum dwellers. They live in crowded highly substandard places where the basic services if at all available, cannot cope with the influx of migrants from rural areas.

Uttara Chauhan and Niraj Lal (1999) studied public-private partnerships for the development of the urban poor, based on experience of the Slum Networking Project in Ahmedabad. Three issues were examined where the first concerns the reasons that impede public-private partnerships. The second was the tardy progress that the central and state governments have made in providing housing and employment to the urban poor. The third issue discussed whether the corporate sector should join hands with government organisations and NGOs for the development of the urban poor. The experiment in Sanjay Nagar throws light on the reasons why such good intentions of the government do not yield results. It also showed that there need a newer approach to solve the unemployment problem. The skills of the unskilled must upgrade so that the unskilled can create for themselves well paying employment opportunities. The government, the NGOs and the corporate sector must work in partnership, with the government playing the facilitator's role.

Chandramouli (2003) presented a profile of Slums in Chennai, the Capital city of the State of Tamil Nadu in South India. It found that a little more than one fourth of the Chennai population lives in Slums. Slums in Chennai are greatly disadvantaged as far as quality of housing and availability of basic amenities like drinking water, electricity, latrines, drainage, non-polluting fuels and the like. Any improvement in the standards of public health will have to start in the Slums. The agenda is long but will have to be addressed in all sincerity.

Karn et al (2003) examined the consequences of socio-economic and environmental factors in terms of income, literacy, sanitation and hygiene for morbidity. The survey covered 1070 households in slums, squatters and Pavement dwellers in Mumbai. The study showed that education level and location of residence have influence on the employment type. Housing conditions differ considerably from pavement dwellers to squatters and slums. Polluted drinking water, insanitary living conditions, poor personal hygiene and food cleanliness are contributed to water related diseases. The impact of poverty and environmental factors highly pronounced between slums and pavement Dwellers. The study revealed that income, literacy, sanitation and personal hygiene have had impact on the morbidity of the people and environmental factors also affecting health status of urban poor. The urban poor need first assurance of being allowed to stay where they are and then provision of basic amenities of toilets, water supply, sewerage and drainage.

Sundari (2003) examined the quality of life of the migrant households in slums of Coimbatore City, Tirupur Town and Chennai City in terms of select parameters. The study revealed that migrant households live in unhygienic and congested places devoid of basic necessities for a healthy life like housing, water supply, drainage and sanitation. Women and children were the worst victims. Physically, mentally and emotionally they are affected. The rehabilitation programme of the Tamil Nadu Slum Clearance Board is totally inadequate in relation to the mushroom growth of slums. Hence, a comprehensive package incorporating measures to improve urban environment and health status should be launched on a massive scale.

Sunil Kumar Karn et al (2003) viewed the consequences of socio-economic and environmental factors in terms of income, literacy, sanitation and hygiene for morbidity. This paper presented and discussed primary data from a survey of 1,070 households in four poor settlements in Mumbai comprising slum- and pavement-dwellers and squatters on the living environment and health conditions. This fact has been substantiated by data that income, literacy, sanitation and personal hygiene have had impact on the morbidity of the people. The impact of poverty and environmental factors has been evidenced by intra-urban-poor gradient seen in four groups of urban poor studied, which is particularly pronounced between slums and pavement-dwellers, the latter has been hit most hard by environmental pollution and lack of basic amenities. Overall, the more the community has gained living stability and socio-economic prosperity, the higher is the concern on environmental pollution and sanitation related factors. The needs of the urban poor and their priorities are seen to be hierarchical. They need first assurance of being allowed to stay where they are and then provision of basic amenities of toilets, water supply, sewerage and drainage.

Chandrasekhar (2005) addressed India's National Slum Policy (NSP) was formulated against the backdrop of inadequate infrastructure availability in Indian slums. Using a unique nationwide dataset on housing conditions and slum infrastructure from India it shed light on how different the rural, non-slum urban poor are from the poor households residing in the urban slums. It found considerable variations in access to services and credit across Monthly Per Capita Expenditure (MPCE) classes. The level of service provision in the slums lies between the conditions in the non-slum urban areas and rural regions. It also analysed the services available in the slums and examines the improvements in the slum conditions over the last five years. The government is active in initiating most of the slum improvements with the NGOs, resident associations active primarily in the water – sanitation sector. Improvements in the living conditions in the slums have left a lot to be desired.

Mony et al (2006) studied the demography, domestic environmental status and maternal health care services in two slums of Vellore town, Tamilnadu. The two slums had comparably secure houses with reasonably good structures. Access to safe water supply, sanitation facilities, and garbage disposal was however very low. A sizeable proportion had inadequate access to high-quality antenatal and obstetric care services. Reliable, local information is essential for managing a decentralized health care system.

Brent Edelman and Arup Mitra (2007) analysed the slum dwellers' access to basic amenities and how they manage to gain access to these amenities. According to the data based on associations between the Indian states' shares of slums, the proportions of notified slums, and the prevailing conditions in slums in terms of basic amenities, political contact is a key factor in this area. The slum survey data (2004-05), which is based on the political economy framework, shows that political contact facilitates easier access to certain facilities, including land tenure and basic amenities. The logit model identifies determinants of political contact by examining social networks and individual endowments. This paper argued that while political accessibility is crucial for the survival strategy, the vulnerability of slum dwellers hardly diminishes in the long run; on the contrary, the political use of slums as "vote banks" perpetuates this vulnerability. Certain findings suggest that strong social networks can prevent low-income households from falling into political traps. It is possible for these households to access amenities and improved living conditions through their own efforts and through social capital, without essentially becoming a part of any political party.

Alison Buttenheim (2008) examined the effect of improved sanitation on child health in urban Bangladesh to assess the relative importance of household versus neighborhood characteristics and of adult latrine usage versus safe disposal of children's feces. Using fixed-effects regression, the change in weight-for-height in 153 children as a function of changes in latrine usage in the surrounding community was calculated. The use of longitudinal data allows children to act as their own controls, a stumbling point of many other sanitation evaluation studies using cross-sectional or case–control methods. Results provide strong evidence that children's toileting matters more than adult toileting behaviour in creating a safe, hygienic environment and reducing diarrheal disease. The concluded that investments in sanitation improvements offer important externalities, and that sanitation programs must encourage the safe disposal of children's feces in order to produce maximum health gains.

Chandrasekhar and Mukhopadhyay (2008) addressed differences in outcomes across households residing in slums and non-slum urban areas of India. Using a nationally representative household data set, it undertook a robust multidimensional evaluation of intra-city differences in well-being. If utility is defined as access to public goods such as water and sanitation, then residents in non-slum urban areas were unambiguously better off than slum dwellers. This finding implied that there was justification for slums garnering a sizable portion of the allocation of water and sanitation programs. On the other hand, the distribution of private goods (monthly per capita expenditure and per capita living area) in non-slum areas did not dominate the distribution of these goods in the slums. In fact, at very low levels of MPCE and per capita living area, the distribution of these private goods in slums dominated the distribution in non-slums. It implies that non-slum residents were not unequivocally better off than slum residents. Since slums are on an average poorer than other urban areas, it may be more pragmatic, therefore, to target policies at slum development. However, such policies would fail to reach the poorest residents of non-slum areas in both large and small cities. The results make the case for a more inclusive policy that targets these groups as well.

Mundu and Bhagat (2008) presented the living conditions of slum dwellers in Mumbai. Most of the slum dwellers in Mumbai lack the basic necessities of life. In spite of many slums got notified by the government, one tap is shared by more than thousand persons in some of the slum compared to an average of 52 persons per tap. Slum dwellers are lacking the access to tap water facility and also they are waiting for hours for the collection of water because of population pressure in these areas. One third of the household have no access to electricity and most of the households share community toilets. The sanitation level of slums is moderately improved as compared with slums with open surface drains. This showed that lots of work still to be done to improve the lives in slums. In spite of several government policies, there is a need to improve the life of slum dwellers through community participation.

Nidhi Kotwal et al (2008) reported a study of Impact of Work and Environment on the Women living in slum areas of Jammu City. The sample for the study consisted of 100 working women from four different slum areas of Jammu City. The results revealed that there is a strong relationship between women's work lives and health. Lack of education compelled women to join low paid sectors. Apart from the general hardships living in an area with a poor environment, Women of slum areas suffered from many disadvantages, they faced a heavier work burden because employment did not free them from responsibility of housework. The dual task (paid and unpaid jobs) and the poor environment became more demanding on the health of the women and the women experienced weakness, fatigue, breathlessness, poor appetite, and frequent illnesses.

Ali and Stevens (2009) summarised the experience of Practical Action in promoting water, sanitation, waste and hygiene-related infrastructure and services in the town of Faridpur, Bangladesh. In addition to the improvement in health and local environment, the project attempted to increase income and employment through the provision and operation of services. Practical Action and its partners have organized community groups and developed participatory slum improvement plans. This then leads to the prioritisation of immediate needs and agreeing roles and responsibilities in the delivery. To address other needs identified in the plans, slum dwellers were encouraged to develop partnerships with the municipality and other service providers. The involvement of people and their empowerment has lead to better use and maintenance of water and sanitation-related infrastructure and services. Community members, once organized have also negotiated better deals with the municipality. However, income and employment from the services, appears to be a more complicated issue in practice as compared to what was planned in the project.

Benjamin Stanwix (2009) examined seven urban slums from Gujarat and Rajasthan describing the current provision of basic services in these areas. It provided a picture of the conditions faced by the average household in these slums, and investigated the underlying relationships between access to infrastructure with health and income of the households. Investigation into correlation between health and infrastructure showed that the household health was correlated with access to basic amenities; those households who do not have access to water, toilet, and drainage (sewerage and storm water) were spending monthly more money on healthcare than those who had access to these services. The latter group also reported higher rate of illness. It was also clear that a relationship did exist between income and access to infrastructure. The poorer households lacked access to water, toilets, drainage, etc. The regression analyzed also showed that spending on household upgrading and acquiring basic amenities was much higher if the house and the land were owned by the family. Spending was also positively correlated with income. It provides strong support to the claim that proper interventions would result in many direct and indirect positive gains.

Karen Tatiana Montiel Lopez (2010) examined the socio-economic and housing characteristics of slum dwellers. In addition, it investigated the main sources of funds for improving slum housing and the financing schemes available in the Ayigya-Zongo and Dakodwom communities in Kumasi. The study adopted the case study method as a way to understand the peculiar situation in the two communities. It revealed that, slum communities suffer from socio-economic problems as well as poor sanitation conditions. These improper conditions challenge the development of communities which may affect the quality life to its residents. It showed that slum dwellers use their own resources to finance housing improvements or acquisition of land. This is because housing financing schemes are almost nonexistent for slum dwellers. It was revealed that the high social cohesion within the communities could facilitate the implementation of government projects for developing affordable housing schemes. Furthermore, government actions have demonstrated that Kumasi is still in a transition between negligence and forced evictions policies for slum control. The study recommended the importance of strengthening local government to lead slum upgrading programmes in the Metropolis. This requires participation of all major stakeholders and capacity building in government institutions and communities.

Prem Kumar (2010) analysed the trend and patterns in the growth of slums in our cities. Data sources for the study are Census of India 1991, 2001 and the 58th round of the NSO on "Condition of Urban Slums". A correlation matrix has been constructed among various indicators. There is significant negative correlation between urban growth rate and the percentage of slum population, implying that cities and towns with high urban growth rates reported low percentage of slum population. It is observed a positive correlation between the percentage of slum population and the percentage of scheduled caste population implying that slum phenomenon is interlinked with socio-economic deprivation. Lack of significant correlation among financial indicators and slum growth rate indicates that slum phenomenon is not related to the financial status of cities/towns. It is largely the relatively better off sections which are able to migrate to urban centres, since moving to cities requires initial staying capacity and certain levels of skill. Certainly, better off sections do not dwell in slums. This may be a reason for the low slum growth rate and the decline in the percentage of slum population. A low slum growth rate vis-à-vis urban growth rate and a decline in the percentage of slum population in the total urban population reveals the exclusionary nature of urban processes manifesting itself in massive slum evictions and low incidence of migration among the lower strata of society. This finding is observed at both macro level and micro level of the city and town. If in-situ slum upgradation and slum improvement programmes were reasons for the observed declining trend of slum growth rate and percentage of slum population, it would have been a model of inclusive urban processes.

Victoria Ijeoma et al (2010) aimed to determine whether income, education, gender, family size, and constraints like high cost of building materials, high house rents, etc. are the factors that contribute to the enugu residents decision to dwell in slums of Agangwu, Ngele-Effor, Ugwu-Aaron, and Ugwu-Bottle. The study revealed that low-income groups could not afford rent for a house in the city due to their low monthly salary (contributed by their educational background), large family size and strict government rules on land and housing, which pushed them to dwell in slums where there were no infrastructural services, no running clean water, no garbage pickups, and sewage services. Therefore, low-income housing was needed in Enugu Metropolitan areas of Nigeria to avoid environmental and health devastations caused by these groups in their slum dwellings, and future research was needed in these areas.

Anuradha Sahay (2012) described quality of life of slum dwellers with the help of composite score index. Spatial analyzed is also done to show segregation and concentration of slums. Various parameters are taken to calculate the levels of quality of life and each parameter given weight-age separately. The results showed that low and very low quality of life exists in the slum. The housing, nutrition, literacy and medical facilities are poor. There exists segregation and concentration of slums in different areas. It showed that the level of disparity is related to the socio-economic and politico-administrative set-up of the city. Hence planning of the region should be done which will remove the disparities in quality of life and create harmonious environment for human resource development.

Ghuncha Firdaus (2012) studied the environmental conditions in and around slum areas and the impact of environmental condition on health profile of the dwellers. The analysed is based on primary data collected at two points of time in ten major slum areas of Aligarh city, India. It revealed that these areas are characterized by complete absence of basic amenities and facilities like drinking water, toilets and bathroom, drainage system and garbage disposal facilities, and no improvement has been observed over the period of seven years. Various infectious non-communicable and communicable diseases especially respiratory infections, tuberculosis and diarhoea and dysentery were observed to be very common health problems that showed positive relationship with the use of traditional fuels, poor personal hygiene and contaminated drinking water respectively. It concluded with policy-oriented discussion of the relationship between urbanization, increasing number of slums and health challenges before the developing nations.

Owoeye and Omole (2012) investigated the sanitary condition of the built environment of residential core of Akure to establish its close relationship with the health situation of its dwellers. Some ecological data involving housing conditions, condition of sanitary facilities; especially the water supply source, sewage and refuse disposal methods, drainage system, kitchen and bathroom facilities were collected. The research population was based on total number of existing buildings from which a sample of 20 per cent was taken for interview. The study revealed that environmental variables were significantly related to health situation of people in the area. The paper suggested some policy guidelines, including redevelopment, upgrading and provision of basic facilities through the Urban Basic Services for the Poor (UBSP) scheme. Besides, regular sanitary inspection, public enlightenment and regular environmental campaign were recommended for sustainable management of the area. It was also expected of the three levels of governments (local, state, and federal) to take active part in the programme particularly in the area of mobilization, training of staff and funding.

Subhash Kumar (2012) attempted to make an economic analysed of environmental and health aspects of the living conditions of the slum dwellers in Visakhapatnam of Andhra Pradesh, India. A multi-stage simple random sampling technique has been employed for the collection of primary data. Two urban slums that is one is notified slum and the rest is non-notified slum with contrasting characteristics have been selected purposively for the study. A total of 500 households have been approached to collect the data. In each slum 250 households are randomly selected for the study. The probit model was used for the factors influencing the household's decision to dwell in the non-notified and notified slums in the study area. The logistic regression model was used for finding out the affect of environmental factors on health of the urban slum dwellers. The results of the logistic regression model indicated that the variables were statistically significant at various levels. It was observed that a majority of the sample households were affected by dust accumulation in the notified slum when compared to non-notified slum. As in the non-notified slum most of the sample households were affected by water pollution, smoke pollution and vector problems than notified slum sample households. The sound pollution was commonly affected by the sample households in both the slums.

Panda and Agarwala (2013) highlighted important issues that impede effective water and sanitation services delivery in the context of experiences and practices captured from two resettlement colonies in Delhi. These areas are deprived of many essential facilities and culpability can be fixed with adequate policy priorities and concomitant public provisioning. There is an acute need to look beyond the existing tiny schemes-centric intervention. A comprehensive agenda for the overall development of slums through a time-barred mission should be formulated with higher allocations for the overall development of water and sanitation facilities in Delhi, especially in urban slums. Issues such as lack of decentralized planning, centralised budgeting, shortage of human resources and poor convergence among implementing agencies need to be surmounted for the smooth implementation of programmes and schemes. The problems need to look at other macro issues such as land tenure rights, livelihood options, education and health facilities in slum colonies whose redress may make water and sanitation schemes little more than just ad hoc interventions.

Bhagat and Malaviya (2013) reviewed on social and environmental aspect of slum dwellers. The study reviewed on environmental and housing conditions, water quality, health and disease related issues. Poor infrastructure facilities such as solid waste disposal, sewage disposal, drainage, public transportation, education and electricity supply which lead to environmental degradation affect all aspects of life. Slums adversely affect the health status of inhabitants due to lack of basic infrastructure, overcrowding, type of fuel used for cooking and health services. These are indeed manifestations of our society and faulty planning. Concrete plans and its effective implementation for the benefits of national growth and migrants are absolutely necessary. The effective policy needs to be framed for the development not only in rural but also in small and medium sized cities. There is an urgent need to generate job opportunities in all regions of India so as to reduce the gap of inequalities. This will assist in combating with poverty, human misery and agony.

2.3.3 REVIEWS ON EDUCATION OF SLUM CHILDREN

There are many studies available and give a general view of the educational problems of the urban slum children. Most of the studies present educational scenario of slum children at field based and concentrate on the specific slums. Few reviews discussed on problem of non-enrolment and dropout, attendance behaviour and access to school of slum children. The findings and observations of these studies are discussed below.

Chitnis and Suvannathat (1984) highlighted the plight of slum children of Bombay. Children living on pavements and in hutments are exposed to harsh heat in summer and to continuous wind and rain during monsoons. For almost four months a year they are often in damp or wet clothing, for weeks on end. Even those who have shelter live nevertheless in places where toilet facilities are negligible, where drains are clogged, flooded and overflowing, where there is no drainage or sanitation at all and certainly without a corner to sit and study or a light to read by at night. The study also finds that children are more often pulled out of the school when the parents move from one place to another for employment or their illegal settlements have been demolished. In most of these cases it leads to dropout. Dropout is considered a phenomenon related to schools that serve poor, the working class and lower middle class. The study also revealed that massive incidence of dropout and failure in Municipal primary schools is due to the combination of poor quality schools and social and economic problems of the families of these children.

Govinda (1995) tried to look into the accessibility of educational facilities to the urban poor and their participation rates. The study points out that about 51 percent of the children are not enrolled in schools and these children are from the slum areas. Major reasons identified for the dropout are elder child is kept at home to look after the younger siblings, the decision is left to the child to go or nor to go to the school, environmental problems as distance to school and danger in crossing roads. It analysed factors like location and environment of the school, type of facilities provided for effectively carrying out the teaching learning process, provision of qualified teachers, levels of efficiency with which the schools are managed and the levels of learning achieved by the learners. It is observed that the above mentioned areas need a considerable improvement. Increased involvement of community based organization, committed volunteers coupled with necessary changes in the bureaucratic procedures and attitude can only improve the educational scene of urban poor in India.

Seetharamu (1998) reviewed the current status of primary education in Bangalore city, taking into account various variables that are considered important to achieve the goal of UEE. The study presents a brief profile of the city. Around 20 percent of the population of Bangalore resides in slum, which is about 410 in number. Three types of slums exist in Bangalore city - the cores are all city centers slums in Southeast are Tamil dominated. There are Muslim dominated slums in this region. The slums on intermediary and peripheral areas especially in Western and North -Western region are Kannad dominated slums. The study pointed out that the problem of primary education in Bangalore City is a problem of slums and marginal population. Around 16 percent of the total population of 6-10 years of age group are still out of the schools. Enrolment of out of school children is a top priority. Enrolment drives should focus their attention towards the slum areas. NGOs involvement for organisation and conduct of Non-Formal Education centers for non-enrolled and dropout children should be planned, supported and encouraged.

Nalini Juneja (2000) analysed as to how the poverty of the poor in Mumbai affects their chances of receiving even a basic education. About 98 percent of the slum dwellers do not have individual water tap and 99 percent of them use open spaces for toilets. As far as education scene of Mumbai city is concerned the study reports that city needs to enroll around 1.8 million children of 6-13 age groups to achieve the goal of UEE. It is argued that the conditions of life of the poor are hard and non-supportive of education. The study tried to review the role of two major organizations namely the Municipal Corporation (MC) and Non-Governmental Organisations towards the goal of UEE in Mumbai city. One of the important developments for the progress of primary education has been observed in the case of Mumbai is that NGO are actively participating along with Municipality for education of the poor. These organizations are trying to improve the access and retention to education by opening non-formal education centres and study classes. They are making school accessible on wheels or a school in bus that park outside the slum areas where, for lack of land, a school cannot be built.

Aggarwal and Sunita Chugh (2003) examined the learners' achievement level of slum children in the government schools and privately run unrecognised schools. This study examined the situation with respect to the home factors, school environment and adequacy of facilities in the selected areas. The association between these factors and learning outcomes is also examined within the stipulated constraints. The achievement results of unrecognised schools with that of Government schools it is cleared that with small and inadequate infrastructure, less financial resources and untrained teachers with low salaries, children of unrecognised schools are performing better than those of the Government schools. The study concluded that, the study makes recommendations to improve the educational attainment among the children living in slums.

Zakir Husian (2005) examined the nature of educational decisions among low income muslims and identify the factors determining such decisions. The primary data was collected on the basis of a household survey of 107 slum dwellers from the Park Circus – Topsia area in Kolkata. Based on the demographic and economic characteristics of slums it was categorised into high, medium and low income slums. The value placed on education and its reason, expenditure pattern on education, opportunity costs of education were discussed. The regression results indicated that opportunity cost exercises a significant influence on education demand, where as income is statistically insignificant for enrollment ratio. The coefficient of the number of school-going children has the anticipated sign. Therefore there is need for creating awareness to improve enrollment of muslims community in India.

Frederick Mugisha (2006) explored patterns of school enrollment comparing urban slum, urban non-slum and rural children. The paper uses data from the Kenya Demographic and Health Survey. The results suggested that school enrollment is higher in urban non-slum than in urban slum areas, and is higher in slums than in rural areas at younger ages. However, this is only true up to age 9 for females and 11 for males, from which school enrollment for slum children declines and the rate of decline is faster than among their rural counterparts. The corresponding ages at which the enrollment among the rural children begins to visibly decline are 13 years for males and 14 years for females. Factors contributing to these results pointed to the poor quality of primary schools in slums, limited access to secondary school for slum children, increased vulnerability to coercion into sexual activity and other ills that hinder school participation, disabling environment at home and increased child labour.

Charles Epari (2007) examined enrolment and gender parity for children attending both public and private schools from Nairobi's slum and non slum areas. Retrospective schooling history data for six years collected within the longitudinal framework of the Nairobi Urban Health Demographic Surveillance System. The model was fitted in the context of Generalized Estimating Equations (GEE) in order to model the probability of attending private school over years and to account for the association among the attendance of the same child over the years. The results suggest that even with free primary education, enrolment in private schools by children from the slums grew. In sharp contrast, more children from the non slum sites attended public schools with those attending private schools. Gender parity is much better for children from the slums attending private schools than their counterparts attending public schools and for those attending both private and public schools in the non slum estates. Pro-poor private schools have a large constituency and complementary role in the provision of primary education to the pupils in informal settlements.

Kumar et al (2007) aimed to trace the spatial pattern of literacy for slums and non-slum population. Intra city analysis has been done for Kolkata, Delhi, Ahmedabad, Jaipur, Ludhiana and Indore. The study find out a major location disparity in literacy. slum population is educationally deprived. Similarly gender still appears to a major issue, female do show their critical condition in literacy not only in slum but also outside the slum in the city. What is needed is the location specific educational development programme with focus on the slums having very low literacy level and high gender disparity in literacy. Slums require special schools where learning and earning can coexist.

Khasnabis and Chatterjee (2007) examined various reasons for poor attendance behavior of students in formal schools. These studies based on random sampling technique 250 students from the slum dominated part of east Kolkata were selected. The logistic regression results indicated that the per capita income, the highest education of the female guardian and the type of school in which the child is pursuing their study are the factors that have some influence on the attendance behaviour of the student. Retaining the students in formal school is far more difficult than enrolling them, particularly if the students are from very poor economic background. The intervention by the NGOs has a positive contribution in meeting this challenge.

Hunt (2008) provided an in-depth review and analysis of literature on dropping out from school, and focuses on children who have gained access, but fail to complete a basic education cycle. The main discussion is around why and how children drop out from school. Here drop out is not presented as a distinct event, but rather a process where a range of supply and demand factors interact to influence schooling access. The paper looked at literature in relation to household, community and social contexts of dropping out, as well as school supply and practices. It also explored what research is saying around pre-cursors to dropping out and factors which may influence retention. Finally, the study identified gaps in research around dropping out and how The Consortium for Educational Access, Transitions and Equity (CREATES) research could address some of these.

Netsayi Mudgege et al (2008) The paper relied on qualitative data collected in Korogocho and Viwandani slum areas in Nairobi, Kenya between October and November 2004. The paper analysed data from individual interviews and focus group interviews and focuses on the narrative of slum dwellers on how insecurity impacts on educational attainment. It mainly focused on threats of physical harm, crime, community and domestic violence. It included insecurity that children suffer from as they go to school, maybe through the use of unsafe routes; insecurity that children feel at school; and the insecurity they suffer from in their homes. As a result policies that address insecurity in slum neighbourhoods can also improve school attendance and performance.

Erten Gokce (2009) carried out study in Ankara, the capital city of Turkey, in order to determined how people living in the slums of Ankara benefit from educational equality. Within the scope of the research, interviews were made with 64 families whose children have been getting education from the primary schools of these parts and the data of the study was collected by the researcher. The results demonstrated that the children getting education in the slums of Ankara cannot experience educational equality and justice. The results of this study showed that the opportunities of the schools in the slums of Ankara are very limited, so the individuals in these districts cannot equally benefit from the education. The families are aware of the problem they are faced with.

Stuart Cameron (2009) described the results from research in the slums of Dhaka. The study draws on the theory of rates of return to education, but also looks beyond that to consider the factors that impede households from accessing the financial and other rewards that supposedly accure from education. In particular, social connections play an important role in getting jobs and realizing other opportunities; and unsurprisingly, gender plays a decisive role in deciding boys' and girls' futures. Although the research uncovered some potential routes through which schooling could reduce poverty, these were not realistically attainable in many cases. The paper considers these results in the light of human and social capital theories and ideas about the reproduction of social class through schooling.

Yuko Tsujita (2009) showed the basic educational status of slum children between 5 and 14 years old. The attendance ratio of slum children is much lower than that of children in Delhi as a whole. Parental perception of education and financing education are the major constraints. Even if children are attending schools, the majority of them are over-aged. There are both demand and supply side reasons for discouraging slum children from attending schooling. As opposed to school based surveys in previous literature, children in slums are more likely to go to government schools rather than low fee paying private schools. Moreover, the existing various government incentive programmes can be improved to reach slum households.

Stuart Cameron (2010) examined survey data from the four slums in Dhaka, it looks at how many children were never enrolled in school, how many dropped out from primary, how many were 'virtually excluded' (attending school but not learning), and how many finished primary but were not able to make the transition to secondary. Using statistical analysis and other information from interviews it also assesses what household and individual factors are associated with each type of exclusion. It emphasised the need for a greater focus on education for the urban poor and considers some policies that could improve the situation.

Valerie Lewis (2010) examined how children living in slums fare in terms of educational attendance and work for pay compared to other urban and rural children. This paper used data from the National Family Health Survey (NFHS) of India, making use of new slum over samples. Several important findings emerge. First, India has made remarkable progress toward universal primary education, reaching nearly 90 per cent attendance. In secondary education, however, slum children are disadvantaged compared to both other urban and rural children slums also experience faster declines in attendance. Both deficit and opportunity cost models are considered as explanations. This research implies further work should be done elucidating the different predictors of primary versus secondary school attendance as well as reasons that slum children are less likely to be attending secondary school.

Sunita Chugh (2011) examined the factors that contribute to dropping out by children at the secondary level. The analysed the marginalized group of children living in slum areas of Delhi, which was conducted during the period from August 2006 - July 2007. The paper revealed that both the family and school related factors were responsible and appeared to be highly correlated with each other. It was also found that adolescents dropout not merely due to poverty and financial constraints but also because the schools did not respond appropriately to their special educational needs forcing them to dropout. This paper proposed that the State needs to adopt a holistic approach to dropout issue and not treat it as merely a discrete problem that can be tackled without reference to the broader socio economic setting and poor delivery of education in which it is rooted. Preventive and restorative approaches, briefly discussed in the paper, are needed to tackle the issue of dropout for children living in slum areas.

2.3.4 HEALTH RELATED STUDIES

The last part of the literature chapter deals with the health problems of slum people. Most of the studies discussed on the magnitude of morbidity, nutritional problems and immunisation status of slum children and health status of slum dwellers. Few selected studies concentrating on the distinct problems are as follows.

Panda et al (1993) studied the health status of under-five children and to observe their immunisation and nutritional status in the "Ash Heap Slum" of Ludhiana, North India. A random cross-sectional survey of 237 under-five years old children in 205 families was selected. It revealed majority of the children belong to migrant families and only 27 per cent of the children were fully immunised while 28 per cent had received no immunisation. About 19 per cent of the children had severe malnutrition, with males and females suffering equally. Diarrhoea and diseases were the major cause of under five morbidity. Provision of basic sanitation and safe water in the urban slum is therefore of a vital necessity.

Akhtar Hussain et al (1999) reported child mortality and its determinants, including the main diseases affecting children and treatments, in the slum population of Dhaka city, Bangladesh. From three slum communities, 1500 households were included in a cross-sectional survey. The most frequent reported causes of deaths were tetanus in infancy and diarrhoea among children. The results showed that gender difference in mortality may have been influenced by the patterns of treatment received during sickness and the choice of treatment was determined by the financial ability of the households. Household income, children's vaccinations, TT immunization of mothers and personal cleanliness appeared to be significantly associated with child mortality. Despite the relatively high vaccination coverage for this population, child mortality remained alarmingly high, indicating that socioeconomic and environmental conditions must be improved to substantially reduce morbidity and mortality in this population.

African Population and Health Research Center (2002) carried out a study on health and livelihood issues facing residents of Nairobi City's informal settlements, and identifies interventions to improve child survival in these communities. The study carried out in-depth interviewed and focused group discussions with mothers, community leaders, service provider and managers of community institutions. Community health concerns and needs revolve around child health, environmental sanitation, and access to basic health care. Most residents depend on expensive profit-driven private health facilities, which mostly operate informally using ill-trained professionals. Health service institutions' key needs include: operational space, qualified health personnel, and diagnostic equipment, particularly laboratory facilities. The settlements are plagued by limited and unreliable livelihood opportunities with majority of residents relying on petty businesses and casual jobs as means of generating income. Access to credit facilities for community members is limited. Institutions working in the communities face serious challenges including lack of financial resources, insecurity and lack of cooperation from the communities.

Kundu (2002) described the health status of slum dwellers in Maharashtra and discusses the constraints in the existing urban health delivery system. It examines the quality of primary services provided by the health posts in urban areas, outlines key areas for policy advocacy and recommends specific steps to improve primary healthcare services. The paper also highlighted the differences within the urban sector. Policies and strategies need to be devised to ensure that health services reach those at the highest risk. In the urban context, the most vulnerable areas are unrecognised slums, temporary settlements and pavement dwellers. Health policy formulation and implementation for the state must take into consideration urban conditions and needs.

Ramamani Sundar and Abhilasha Sharma (2002) observed the patterns of morbidity and healthcare utilisation by the urban poor living in slums and resettlement colonies in Delhi and Chennai, and compare the health status of the two segments. The findings of the survey indicate that people living in resettlement colonies have a better health status than the slum dwellers. As far as utilisation of health facilities is concerned, in spite of the presence of health facilities nearby a significant proportion of the sample population living in the slums and colonies do not seek treatment for all their illnesses, particularly the old people. It revealed that the sample households do incur a substantial expense on the treatment of ailments even if the treatment is sought from a government facility. Thus, substantial health gains could be achieved either by improving the environmental and sanitation conditions in the existing slums or by relocating the slum dwellers in the resettlement colonies. Thus, there is a need to strengthen the public health services in urban areas especially for the slum dwellers.

Neeraj and Sanjay (2003) measured the incidence of malnourishment among under-five children in slums in Mumbai and compare it to the incidence in Jawhar tehsil of Thane district known for high levels of malnourishment. It observed that there were socio cultural and behavioural barriers like female illiteracy, poor economic status of women etc which affect the nutritional status of children. The study showed that seasonal wasting incidence is likely to be higher in girls. Malnourishment is very likely to occur when insufficient incomes co-exist with poor coverage of basic amenities and health services. But at the same time urban slum dwellers are undernourished and the proportion was very high in slum areas. Based on nutritional indicators the study showed that severe malnourishment was found to be higher in Mumbai than in Jawaharlal colony. To conclude a policy that combines income improvement with greater public health facilities and legislation is most likely to succeed in Mumbai.

Jane Pryer et al (2003) examined the impact of workdays off due to illness on the financial status and livelihoods of poor slum dwellers in Dhaka, Bangladesh. Data on illness and socioeconomic status were collected in a panel survey with monthly rounds. The researcher contacted over 12,000 individuals during a 12-month period and 2,682 adults had taken workdays off due to illness. Households reporting illness in adults had lower income and expenditures than the remainder. They were less likely to have loans and less likely to be members of credit organisations. Where adults had taken time off work due to illness, households reported a deficit in their financial situation, reduced their expenditure, took out loans or mortgages, changed their work or begged. Particular households may be vulnerable to adult ill health. When ill health prevents an adult earner from working, the household financial situation deteriorates, and strategies are used to offset the effect. It is likely that adult illness is a major contributor to chronic poverty.

Ghosh and Shah (2004) examined nutritional problems in urban slum children. The diets and nutritional status of urban slum children in India is far away from being satisfactory. The nutritional status of slum children is worst amongst all urban groups and is even poorer than the rural average. Urban migration has not provided them salvation from poverty and undernutrition. Another distressing feature is the lack of any significant improvement over the years in this population. Most common causes of malnutrition include faulty infant feeding practices, impaired utilization of nutrients due to infections and parasites, inadequate food and health security, poor environmental conditions and lack of proper child care practices. High prevalence of malnutrition among young children is also due to lack of awareness and knowledge regarding their food requirements and absence of a responsible adult care giver. With increasing urban migration in the years ahead, the problem of malnutrition in urban slums will also acquire increasing dimension unless special efforts are initiated to mitigate the health and nutrition problems of the urban poor. Improving nutritional status of urban poor requires a more direct, more focused, and more integrated strategy.

Gulis (2004) described the health status of people living in the slums of Nairobi. It was designed as a cross sectional study based on data from visitors at a clinic at Trnava University located in Mukuru slum in Nairobi. There were about 16,000 visits registered at Mary Immaculate Clinic of Trnava University in Nairobi during 2 years of operation. A random 5 per cent sample was drawn from the paper-card database of this clinic to assess basic characteristics and health complaints of visitors. Both self-reported health complaints and diagnoses written by physicians were used to assess health status of participants. The major self-reported health complaints of visitors were cough, abdominal pain, and headache for both sexes. The most frequent diagnoses were consequently virosis, acute respiratory infections, and bronchitis. Differences in health complaints by slums were observed and are described herein. The major health complaints and diagnoses in addition to the differences in health complaints and diagnoses by slum show that environmental conditions can have major influences on health status. Therefore, environmental improvements are important in the improvement of health status. A very high prevalence of respiratory complaints and gastrointestinal problems signify that improvements in air pollution reduction, drinking water provision, and waste management in slums can lead to more significant and sustainable improvements in health status than just simple treatment. This fact should be taken into account when planning future relief programs.

Abdus Salam et al (2006) assessed the association between spousal violence and women's reproductive health. Data was collected from 496 women. Subjects were chosen from eight randomly selected urban slums from four metropolitan cities. Spousal violence was significantly higher amongst the group of less educated women who had been in several marriages; indicating that the social and behavioral traits of women act as catalysts for spousal violence. It injuries adversely affect the health and well-being of women. More than three-quarters of physically violated women suffered injuries as a result of this violence. More than 80 per cent of sexually violated women complained of pelvic pain, more than 5 per cent reported reproductive tract infections, and more than 50 per cent reported symptoms of irritable bowel syndrome. The findings of this study may enhance understanding of the impact of spousal violence against women and their reproductive health and therefore highlight the importance of spousal violence prevention measures. Increasing the awareness and understanding of the relationship between violence against women and reproductive health could be achieved if lawyers, researchers, clinicians, practitioners, and government workers from multiple disciplines and agencies worked together.

Pryer et al (2006) analysed on adult illness in Dhaka slum households. Cluster analysis was used to identify relatively homogenous groups within Dhaka slum households, who report similar patterns of livelihood. Four groups emerged which may be summarised as "self employed", "casual unskilled", "female headed" and "casual skilled" households on the basis of their socio-economic, demographic and occupational characteristics. The "self employed" and "casual skilled" groups were better off in terms of income, assets and creditworthiness. The greatest burden of adult illness fell in the "casual unskilled" and "female headed". The prevalence of sickness-induced loss of employment was found to be very high in the Dhaka slums, represented substantial loss of earnings and was disproportionately borne by the poorest households. Programmes, which mitigate the adverse effects of adult ill health on household economies, might help break the cycle of ill health and poverty, which characterise many urban slum households, and could help reduce inequalities between livelihood groups.

Riley et al (2007) discussed observations made in one slum community of 58,000 people in Salvador, the third largest city in Brazil, to highlight the existence of a spectrum and burden of chronic illnesses not likely to be detected by the formal sector health services until they result in complications or death. Lack of health-related data from slums could lead to inappropriate and unrealistic allocation of health care resources by the public and private providers. Similar misassumptions and misallocations are likely to exist in other nations with large urban slum populations. Continued neglect of ever-expanding urban slum populations in the world could inevitably lead to greater expenditure and diversion of health care resources to the management of end-stage complications of diseases that are preventable. A new approach to health assessment and characterization of social-cluster determinants of health in urban slums is urgently needed.

Jurg Graf et al (2008) studied factors that presumably affect the incidence of diarrhoea among young children in urban slums in developing countries: consumption of safe drinks, hygiene behaviour, cleanliness of household surroundings and the quality of raw water. Beliefs concerning the causes of diarrhoea were also related to health-improving behaviour, namely the application of the water-treatment method solar water disinfection (SODIS) and hygiene behaviour. A survey was conducted in a shanty town in Nairobi, Kenya. Analysis with regression models revealed that two out of the four postulated factors were significant: children have a lower risk of contracting diarrhoea when they consume high percentages of safe drinks and live in households with good hygiene. As regards beliefs, it found that biomedical knowledge of children's diarrhoea as well as the perceived social norm for treating water was associated with the use of SODIS and good hygiene.

Haque and Rashid (2009) conducted a cross-sectional study at a purposively selected Mohakhali slum known as Sat-tala Basti of Dhaka city with a view to assess the nutritional status of women of reproductive age living in the slum. A total of 510 slum women were interviewed and their anthropometric measurements were taken. A large number of respondents were in the age group of 15 to 24 years. Majority of the respondents and their husband were illiterate. The mean Body Mass Index (BMI) of the respondents was 19.2 (±2.4) and about one-third of the respondents were malnourished. The nutritional status determined by BMI was not found significantly associated with education and occupation of the respondents, but monthly family income showed a positive relationship with BMI of the respondents. This study provided a vivid picture of the nutritional status of the slum mothers and could provide help to the concerned authority in their policy making and planning to alleviate the problem.

Lewis (2009) seeked to quantify disadvantages are faced by children living in slums in India. It is found that slum infants and children face higher mortality than other urban children but lower mortality than rural children. If family background is taken, these differences disappear entirely. Slum children are no more likely to be malnourished or suffer acute illness symptoms than other children. Slum children are indistinguishable from other urban children until age 14, at which point they become much less likely to be in school than either rural or other urban children. A combination of a vibrant informal economy in slums that provides incentives for children to work and a deficit of government run high schools for children to attend. The results indicated that slums are a difficult and complex phenomenon to measure, not a homogenous set of neighbourhoods. In some ways slums disadvantage residents, but in other ways slums may provide advantages compared to rural residence.

Neeraj Srivastava, Shally Awasthi and Girdhar Agarwal (2009) assessed distribution of Neonatal Illnesses And Different Health Providers Sought(NIDHPS), distribution of out-of-pocket expenditures by type of illness and type of health provider sought and socio-economic distribution of neonatal illnesses, care-seeking behaviour and out-of pocket expenditures. Per-protocol analysis was performed. Five hundred and ten neonates were enrolled and 481were followed-up. More than half parents of neonates reported at least one symptom of illness. Of these one-fourth neonates had illnesses with at least one reported Integrated Management of Neonatal and Childhood Illnesses (IMNCI) danger sign. Community based Nongovernment Dispensers (NGDs) were leading health providers. Mean monthly income of families was Rs.2804 and mean out-of-pocket expenditure on neonatal illness was Rs.547.5 and mean out-of-pocket expenditure for hospitalization was RS.4993. All hospitalizations were for IMNCI illnesses. Neonates from lower income strata were less likely to receive any medical care and were also less likely to be seen by a Government provider. Also, since NGDs, half of which could be unqualified are leading health providers, qualified medical care-seeking for sick newborns should be promoted in urban Lucknow.

Mihir and Geeta (2010) studied the socio-demographic and environmental profiles as well as magnitude of morbidity among urban slum dwellers. The cross sectional study had been carried out between January 2000 and December 2000 on non-randomly selected 1,389 slum dwellers of Ahmedabad. General physical examinations and history of illness present in previous two weeks were recorded. There were no sanitary latrines and drainage facilities at studied slum. The literacy rate was higher among males. The morbidity rate for both sexes was 30.88 per cent. Anemia was found in females of age group of 15 to 44 years. Respiratory tract infections and diarrhea were present in studied population. The incidence rates for respiratory tract infections and diarrhea were found higher among 0 to 4 year age group children. Slum clinic or mobile clinic van should be arranged for treatment of common morbidities and health promotional activities.

Khan (2010) investigated the economic consequences of health shocks and coping mechanisms for poor urban households in Bangladesh using longitudinal household survey and qualitative data. Two measures of health shocks are included in the empirical analysis: a recent death of a household member and a recent serious illness that incapacitates a household member. The findings confirm that the effects of health shocks on income differ between earned and unearned income. The serious illness only affects earned income negatively and significantly suggesting intra household labour adjustment cannot compensate lost income though it can compensate lost worked hours. The regression results reject the hypothesis of consumption smoothing in the face of a death of a household member. On the other hand, results suggest that coping strategies lead households in a vulnerable situation.

Kirti Ghei (2010) examined the association between presence of an Urban Health Center (UHC) in proximity to a slum and immunization status of slum children in a city in India. Data were obtained from a baseline survey conducted by the United Stats Agency for International Development Environmental Health Project in 2005 in slums in Agra. The study population consisted of 1728 children aged 10 to 23 months. Information about children's immunization was obtained from interviews with mothers aged 15 to 44 years. Immunization status of children was measured as complete, partial and not. Adjusted relative risk ratios compared children receiving complete or partial immunization with those not immunized. Adjusted models showed that presence of a UHC within 2 km of a slum was associated with more than twice the likelihood of children being completely or partially immunized. It found that presence of a UHC was positively associated with immunization status of children in slums. These results suggest a need for greater public attention to expand coverage of slums through UHCs.

Sengupta et al (2010) determined the prevalence and risk factors of under-nutrition amongst under-five children living in an urban slum of Ludhiana; a cross-sectional survey of 200 randomly selected under-five children was carried out. The median weight-for-age, height-for-age and weight-for-height of the NCHS standard were used as reference anthropometric indices. Female children, children aged 48-59 months, children born to older mothers aged 30-49 years, children with >3 siblings, low birth weight, those exclusively breast-fed for >6 months or <4 months, having an illiterate mother or unskilled labourer father were observed to be at the highest risk of being under-nourished. Birth spacing of <2 years, incomplete vaccination status, frequent infections and worm infestation were also found to be important predisposing factors for childhood malnutrition. The study demonstrated the multiple risk factors for childhood malnutrition, requiring a multi-pronged and multi-sectoral approach in the fight against the silent killer of childhood malnutrition.

Deepak Mili (2011) assessed the access to health services by the migrant population settled in Shivaji Nagar Slum of Mumbai. A cross-sectional study was conducted. Purposive sampling was used to select the households. The findings revealed that families with low income preferred to go to Brihanmumbai Municipal Corporation (BMC) hospitals where as families with more income to go to general practitioners. Respondents who had education up to secondary level preferred to go to the general practitioner where as those with education level higher than secondary preferred to go to BMC or private hospitals. From the issues that emerged from the study and recognizing the paramount importance of health in the well-being of the people, it is crucial that policy action be taken to improve health services for migrant populations who live in the unauthorized slums.

Benta Abuya et al (2012) determined effect of mother's education on child nutritional status of children living in slum settings. Data were obtained from Nairobi Urban Health and Demographic Surveillance System (NUHDSS) on nutritional status of children aged 0-42 months. Binomial and multiple logistic regressions were used to estimate the effect of education. Maternal education is a strong predictor of child stunting with some minimal attenuation of the association by other factors at maternal, household and community level. Other factors including at child level: child birth weight and gender; maternal level: marital status, parity, pregnancy intentions, and health seeking behaviour; and household level: social economic status are also independently significantly associated with stunting. Given that stunting is a strong predictor of human capital, emphasis on girl-child education may contribute to breaking the poverty cycle in urban poor settings.

Suz (2012) studied the relationship between maternal education and child health in India, focusing on the differences between rural, urban, and urban slum areas. For rural and urban areas increasing maternal education significantly improves child health, with the effect of an additional year of education significantly higher in urban areas than in rural areas. This effect does not hold in slum areas. Children of mother's with no education do significantly better in slums than in rural areas but education affect health substantially less in slums than in rural or urban areas. Only for women with high levels of education, more than 10 years, is the effect of education on child health statistically significant. This effect masks large difference between boys and girls with the marginal effect of education for boys close to zero.

Kiranmai et al (2012) examined women's health status in slums of Visakhapatnam. A convenience sample of 100 female participants ranging from 18-69 years of age was selected. Participants are living in kachha houses with an average of 3 children per household. They were educated till primary and secondary levels, lived in unhygienic and difficult conditions, worked in the informal service sector and consumed a diet low in protein. Health concerns included a variety of acute and chronic conditions and difficulties accessing health was mainly due to poverty. The results indicated that the perceived health condition by the women is good as a fact that in spite of many health effects they were not in medication and doesn't visit a doctor.

Hmwe Hmwe Kyu (2013) examined the contextual influences of urban slum residency on infant mortality and child stunting over and above individual and household characteristics and identified factors that might modify any adverse effects. Data was obtained from Demographic and Health Surveys conducted in 45 countries between 2000 and 2009. The respondents were women (15–49 years) and their children (0–59 months). Results showed that living in a slum neighborhood was associated with infant mortality irrespective of individual and household characteristics and this risk was attenuated among children born to women who had received antenatal care from a health professional. It indicated that increasing child age exacerbated the risk for stunting associated with slum residency. The findings suggest that improving material circumstances in urban slums at the neighborhood level as well as increasing antenatal care coverage among women living in these neighborhoods could help reduce infant mortality and stunted child growth.

Malaviya and Bhagat (2013) studied the health related risk factors among the slum dwellers of Muthi area of Jammu city. Most of the slum dwellers were poor migrant people of other states come in search of job. Single room accommodation was highly prominent in these slum-dwellers due to low income. All the houses in the locality of present study were kutcha houses, the condition of the floor was found to be miserable as more than fifty percent dwellers had rough and damp type of floor where cracks and crevices were common. The littered night soil in and around slum area, overflowing sewage water drains, open dumping of solid waste were the chief causes of environmental degradation in the locality. For minor illnesses or any other health related problems, most of the households preferred traditional medicine or therapy. Unhygienic conditions, open defecation system, burning of wood inside ill ventilated rooms, ill-habits such as chewing of tobacco, drinking, least care about health, domiciliary deliveries etc. are the major risk factors to the people of study area. There is strong urge to deals with slums in a constructive ways otherwise problems of slums will deals with citites in a destructive way.

Ronak Patel et al (2013) sought to determine the monetary cost of diarrhoea to urban slum households in Kaula Bandar slum in Mumbai, India. The study also tested the hypotheses that the cost of water and sanitation infrastructure may be surpassed by the cumulative costs of diarrhoea for households in an urban slum community. The baseline survey was administered to a random sample of households. The systematic longitudinal survey was administered to every available household in the community with a case of diarrhoea for a period of 5 weeks. For the longitudinal survey, all available household in Kaula Bandar was approached and consenting adults were included. The direct cost of medical care for having at least one person in the household with diarrhoea was Rs.205. Adding an average loss of Rs.55 per household from lost wages and monetising lost productivity from homemakers gave a total loss of Rs.409 per household. During the 5-week study period, this community lost an estimated Rs.163,600 due to diarrhoeal illness. The lack of basic water and sanitation infrastructure is expensive for urban slum households in this community. Financing approaches that transfer that cost to infrastructure development to prevent illness may be feasible. These findings along with the myriad of unmeasured benefits of preventing diarrhoeal illness add to pressing arguments for investment in basic water and sanitation infrastructure.

Sarkar et al (2013) described the morbidity experience of children living in semi-urban slums of a southern Indian city. A total of 176 children were recruited pre-weaning from four geographically adjacent, semi-urban slums located in the western outskirts of Vellore, Tamil Nadu for a study on water safety and enteric infections and received either bottled or municipal drinking water based on their area of residence. Children were visited weekly at home and had anthropometry measured monthly until their second birthday. A total of 3932 episodes of illness were recorded during the follow-up period, resulting in an incidence of 12.5 illnesses and child-year, with more illness during infancy than in the second year of life. Respiratory, mostly upper respiratory infections and gastrointestinal illnesses were most common. The study found a high burden of childhood diseases and malnutrition among urban slum dwellers in southern India. Frequent illnesses may adversely impact children's health and development, besides placing an additional burden on families who need to seek healthcare and find resources to manage illness.

2.4 CONCLUSION

These review of literature as a secondary sources have provided tremendous help in building the theoretical base of the research study and helped the researcher in conceptualising problem. Many studies were also conducted in various parts of the world at various dimensions on health, education and living conditions in slums. But none of these studies has concentrated on all the three concepts as an integrated one. Since an integrated analysis of three aspects is necessary for the slum demolition. The forth coming chapters initiate towards this work lane.

Chapter III

OVERVIEW OF URBAN SLUM

3.1 INTRODUCTION

In the previous chapters, the researcher discussed about the existing literatures of dwellers of slum area. The present chapter concentrates on the profile of study area. It is devoted to discuss the profile of study area and the growth of slum areas in global, national and region level in India.

3.2 PROFILE OF SALEM DISTRICT

3.2.1 HISTORY AND GEOGRAPHY

The third century BC marks the arrival of Jainism and Buddhism in the district of Salem. Around the beginning of the Christian era, the existence of an economically and culturally advanced society in the Salem district two thousand years ago was evident from the discovery of silver coins of the Roman emperor Tiberices Claudices Nero in Koneripatti of Salem in the year 1987. The rule of the Pandiyan dynasty over Salem district starts in the second century A.D. The fourth century A.D. witnessed the rise of the Pallava dynasty in the district of Salem and in the sixth century the rise of the Saivite principle was witnessed. The tenth century marks the rise of the Chola dynasty in this district and in the twelfth century the Hoysala Empire ruled over Salem. In the fourteenth century, the district of Salem went under the rule of the Vijayanagar Empire. The fifteenth and the sixteenth century saw the rule of the Chalukyas and the Madurai Nayaks over the district of Salem respectively. The eighteenth century saw the rule of Hyder Ali and then his son Tipu Sultan over Salem and in this century Salem slipped into the hands of the British East India Company until India became independent in the year 1947.

3.2.2 LOCATION AND AREA

The entire Salem district falls under the North Western Zone of Tamilnadu. Salem district is one of the largest districts in Tamil Nadu. It is bounded on the North by Dharmapuri District, Namakkal and Erode districts in South, the Western Ghats in the West and on the East by Villupuram district. Salem district is situated between 11°14 and 12°53 North latitude and 77°44 and 78°50 East longitudes.

3.2.3 RAINFALL

The average annual rainfall of Salem District is 843 millimeter. The rainfall is well distributed between May and November, while in the month of September the intensity of rainfall is high.

3.2.4 TEMPERATURE

The temperature varies from 19.1C to 39.5° with the maximum temperature prevailing during the month of April and May i.e. 39.5° to 39.1° and the minimum temperature in the month of November.

3.2.5 ADMINISTRATIVE DIVISIONS

The administrative classification of Salem District consists of four revenue divisions, nine taluks, twenty blocks, five municipalities, 22 town panchayats, 636 revenue villages and 385 village panchayats respectively. The District of Salem was divided into nine taluks namely Attur, Mettur, Omalur Sankari, Salem, Yercaud, Gangavalli, Idappadi and Vazhapadi. The above mentioned division was made for easy and efficient functioning of the district affairs.

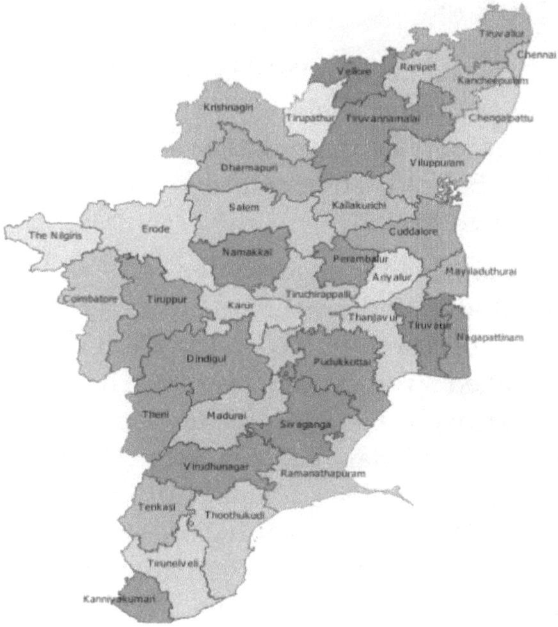

Figure 3.1 : District Map of Tamil Nadu

Source : https://www.tn.gov.in/DistrictMap

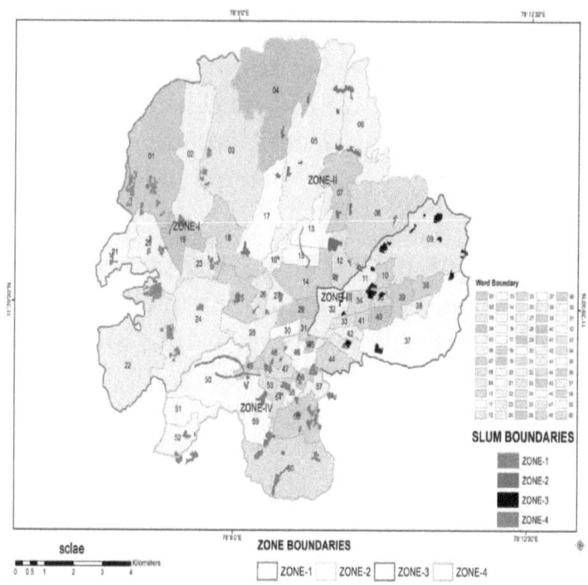

Figure 3.2 : Zone Wise Slums Area in Salem City

Source : Slume Clearance Board, Salem

3.2.6 POPULATION

In 2011, Salem had population of 3,480,008 of which male and female were 1,780,569 and 1,699,439 respectively. There was change of 15.37 percent in the population compared to population as per 2001. In the previous census of India 2001, Salem District recorded increase of 17.20 percent to its population compared to 1991.

The initial provisional data suggest a density of 663 in 2011 compared to 575 of 2001. Total area under Salem district is of about 5,245 sq.km. Average literacy rate of Salem in 2011 were 73.23 compared to 65.09 of 2001. If things are looked out at gender wise, male and female literacy were 80.70 and 65.43 respectively. For 2001 census, same figures stood at 74.39 and 55.20 in Salem District. Total literate in Salem District were 2,311,715 of which male and female were 1,300,874 and 1,010,841 respectively. In 2001, Salem District had 1,734,442 in its total region. With regards to Sex Ratio in Salem, it stood at 954 per 1000 male compared to 2001 census figure of 929. The average national sex ratio in India is 940 as per latest reports of Census 2011 Directorate.

In census enumeration, data regarding child under 0-6 age were also collected for all districts including Salem. There were total 323,102 children under age of 0-6 against 351,859 of 2001 census. Of total 323,102 male and female were 168,560 and 154,542 respectively. Child Sex Ratio as per census 2011 was 917 compared to 851 of census 2001. In 2011, Children under 0-6 formed 9.28 percent of Salem District compared to 11.67 percent of 2001. There was net change of -2.39 percent in this compared to previous census of India.

Salem District population constituted 4.82 percent of total Tamil Nadu population. In 2001 census, this figure for Salem District was at 4.82 percent of Tamil Nadu population. All details regarding Salem District have been processed by us after receiving from Govt. of India. We are not responsible for errors to population census details of Salem District.

Table 3.1: Distribution of Population

Description	2011	2001
Actual Population	3,480,008	3,016,346
Male	1,780,569	1,563,633
Female	1,699,439	1,452,713
Population Growth	15.37 per cent	17.20 per cent
Area Sq. Km	5,245	5,245
Density/km^2	663	575
Proportion to Tamil Nadu Population	4.82 per cent	4.83 per cent
Sex Ratio (Per 1000)	954	929
Child Sex Ratio (0-6 Age)	917	851
Average Literacy	73.23	65.09
Male Literacy	80.70	74.39
Female Literacy	65.43	55.20
Total Child Population (0-6 Age)	323,102	351,859
Male Population (0-6 Age)	168,560	190,129
Female Population (0-6 Age)	154,542	161,730
Literates	2,311,715	1,734,442
Male Literates	1,300,874	1,021,772
Female Literates	1,010,841	712,670
Child Proportion (0-6 Age)	9.28 per cent	11.67 per cent
Boys Proportion (0-6 Age)	9.47 per cent	12.16 per cent
Girls Proportion (0-6 Age)	9.09 per cent	11.13 per cent

Source : http://censusindia.gov.in

3.2.7 THE STANLEY RESERVOIR

An architectural marvel and important land mark in the Mettur Division of Salem, it is the heart that pumps the life giving water to the farmers of the Cauvery basin who suffer the vagaries of Indian monsoons. The sixteen Gates is an Engineering master-piece and regulates the flow of water released from the Mettur Dam to the lower reaches covering the paddy fields in the eight districts of Salem, Erode, Namakkal, Karur, Tiruchirapalli, Thanjavur, Thiruvarur and Nagapattinam.

3.2.8 THE SALEM STEEL PLANT

This was an ambitious project started with a view to utilise the locally available iron-ore from Kanchamalai to produce steel. Now it is a public sector company engaged in rolling out cast steel blacks into sheets of required dimensions by cold and hot extrusion methods. Mineral Deposits: The district is rich in mineral deposits like Magnesite, Bauxite, Granite, Limestone, Quartz and Iron ore. Allied industries like Magnesite mining, cement manufacture, refractory bricks manufacture, Aluminium smelting etc thrive well.

3.2.9 EMPLOYMENT IN AGRICULTURE

Agriculture and allied sector offer employment opportunities in the rural areas. Ploughing, sowing and harvesting are the main avenues of agricultural employment. The rate of wages paid to the agricultural employees is not based on the wages fixed by the Government. But at present lump sum amount is paid to the agriculture labourers in rural areas.

3.2.10 AGRICULTURE PRODUCES

Many agricultural products from Salem have a wide spread market throughout the country. Mango fruits from Salem are enjoyed and much sought after, specially the variety Malgoa-which is the pride of Salem besides a number of other newly introduced hybrid varieties. Tapioca locally known as Maravalli (or) Kuchi Kilangu is extensively cultivated by the farmers of Salem. Salem holds a monopoly in Tapioca production. The tubers are used primarily to produce starch. A variety of food items like chips, forums, papads, Noodles and vermicelli are also produced from tapioca. Tapioca and castor Research centre functioning in Salem is engaged in Research and Development activities to produce high yielding and disease resistant varieties

Sago-serve is run by the Government, to provide a competitive market where farmers gain a broader profit margin without to hassle of the middle-men dealings. Coffee the slopes of Yercaud hills are covered with vast plantations of coffee, shaded by silver Oak trees, Narasus coffee – a popular brand has its origin in Salem. Sandal wood: Santalum album species of Sandal wood grows in the forests of Salem. They fetch high prices as their heart woods yield high oil content about 6 per cent (average). The Mysore Sandal soap company is a noted buyer of Sandal woods from Salem.

3.2.11 ANIMAL HUSBANDRY

The Sheep Research station located at Mecheri in Mettur, developed and introduced the popular Mecheri Breed. The breed is popular among the farmers and is reared mainly for meat purposes.

3.2.12 DAIRY

Salem Diary has an impressive milk production and the district stands first in milk production. A variety of milk products have been introduced by the Diary recently and are effectively marketed.

3.2.13 COTTAGE INDUSTRIES

Production of un-bleached sugar-vellam or Nattu Sarkarai is a major cottage industry among the sugarcane cultivators of Salem. Rope making is another major cottage industry. Ropes are made by people out of the fibres of coconut, Aloe vera, Cotton, Jute. Salem has a sizeable weaver population and weaving is an important house hold industry here. Both silk and cotton fabrics woven in Salem find popular market throughout the State. The Ammapet weaver's co-operative society has a turnover of 2.40 crores and its main products are cotton sarees, bed sheets, towels, silk sarees and dhotis. Silver works: Making of Silver ornaments and artifacts by hand work is an important cottage industry in Salem. Silver anklets made in Salem are popular throughout the country.

3.2.14 CINEMA THEATRES

Salem was once a popular Tinsel town where the earlier Tamil movies were created in the Modern Theatres. The people of Salem are great movie viewers and the popularity of cinema is evident from the fact that there are nearly a hundred and odd Theatres in the district-perhaps the largest in any district.

3.2.15 TEMPLES

Many temples with intricate sculptures and imposing towers are found in the district of Salem, built by indigenous ruler's centuries before the British era. Some of the popular temples are the Taramangalam Shivan Temple in Omalur and the Sukavaneswarar temple, Kottai Mariamman temple, Murugan, Muniappan, Parsanna Venkatesha Perumal temple in Salem.

3.2.16 FORTS

Forts had existed in Salem town and Omalur said to have been visited by Tipu Sultan. Uncared for, not even the ruins of these monuments remain to be seen today. However at Sankagiri an impressive fort is seen on a hillock, with its elaborate and massive ramparts running all the way up the hill. This fort is said to have been the holding of Theeran Chinnamalai an indigenous warrior who fought against British oppression.

3.2.17 TOURISM

Salem is also the headquarters of Salem District. Salem is at the base of the renowned tourist destination of Yercaud hills, which offers breathtaking views both during the ride up the hill and from the peak. The cool and mild climate prevailing here makes it an ideal summer retreat. There are also remote sites of beauty such as Kiliyur Falls. Yercaud is at an altitude of 1600 m above mean sea level. There are people from different states of India settled in Salem. The word "Salem" literally means, "Surrounded by hills". The city of Salem is surrounded by several ranges of hills, including the Shevaroys and Yercaud hills. Coffee, spices like cardomom, pepper, fruits like "Kamala" Orange, butter fruit, Jack fruit are grown in Yercaud and find good market. The city is surrounded by an amphitheatre of hills, the Nagaramalai in the north, the Jeragamalai in the south, the Kanjanamalai on the west and Godumalai on the east. It is divided by the Thirumanimuthar in the main division. The fort is the oldest place of the town.

3.2.18 HILLS

Salem district with an area of 8649 sq. km is extensively covered with hilly ranges and rocks with undulating plains ranging between 152 and 366 metres.

3.2.19 RIVERS

The important rivers in the district are Cauvery, Vasishta Nadhi, the Sweda Nadhi and the South Pennar.

3.2.20 HEALTH

This district enjoys a temperate climate which is generally good to healthy living. The hilly areas were however infected with Malaria but due to the operations of the National Malaria Eradication programme this scourage has been completely eradicated. The tribal and other people living in the hills are now completely free from Malaria. The achievements under Public Health Schemes during the last 20 years are noteworthy. Under Guinea Worm Eradication scheme, wells were chlorinated and health staff were appointed for this purpose.

In Salem District One Head Quarters Hospital, Six Taluk Hospital, Two Non-Taluk Hospitals and One Government Dispensary are functioning in Medical and Rural Health Services side.

Table 3.2 : Details of Salem Head Quarters Hospital

Type of Government Hospital	No's	Name of Hospital
Government Head Quarters Hospital	1	Mettur Dam
Taluk Hospitals	6	Government Hospitals, Attur, Omalur, Sankari, Edappadi, Yercaud and Gangavalli
Non Taluk Hospitals	2	Government Hospitals, Vembadithalam & Jalakandapuram
Government Dispensary	1	Kariakoil

Source : Health and Family Welfare Department, Government of Tamil Nadu.

3.2.21 POVERTY RATIOS AND INTENSITY

Over the years, implementation of Anti-Poverty Programmes such as NREP, RLEGP, IRDP, JRY, SGRY and SGSY is yet to make a dent in rural poverty and indebtedness. This situation needs to be redressed quickly. In Salem District, it is estimated that 2.04 lakhs people out of the total of 30.66 lakhs live below the poverty line and 7.54 lakhs people belong to the working class. So they are in need of wage employment thoroughout the year. Schemes such as SGRY, NREGS provide employment to rural people but it is not sufficient to provide employment to all needy rural people because of limited financial allocation.

3.2.22 MIGRATION PATTERN

Migration is a common phenomena in the Salem District. Migration that occurs among the public is classified as follows.

1. Migration from the rural areas to a nearby Industrial Town or City seeking employment opportunities.
2. Migration from the villages to the nearby towns seeking education facilities to the children and in search of basic amenities. Among these two categories, migration seeking employment opportunities stands first.

3.2.23 SEASONS OF MIGRATION

Thousands of people, predominantly comprising agricultural labourers migrate to neighbouring districts and state during the agricultural lean season from the month of March – May villages move especially to Thirupur, Coimbatore, Chennai & Bangalore, the metropolitan city in search of livelihood.

3.2.24 RURAL TO URBAN MIGRATION

This type of migration occurs in search of Medical, Educational and Job opportunities. Since the rate of migrations varies from time to time, rate of migration cannot be accurately estimated.

3.2.25 URBAN TO RURAL AREAS MIGRATION

The rate of Migration from urban to rural areas is very low in Salem District.

3.2.26 MIGRATION WITHIN DISTRICT

This type of migration is felt among the people in Government Services and the small-scale businessmen. The rate is very low.

3.2.27 MIGRATION FROM OUTSIDE THE DISTRICT

Migration from outside the Salem district occurs only in the student community. So rating in this category is also very low.

3.2.28 MIGRATION OUTSIDE STATES, ITS SEASONAL AND REGIONAL PATTERN OF OUT-MIGRATION AND IN MIGRATION

Migration outside the states only occurs during the period of Harvest. The small Farmers and the landless labourers migrate to other states seeking wage employment opportunities. Those people are usually engaged in quarries, Road works, and Building works, etc., But this migration is only seasonal. But the rate of migration from the other states to Salem is very low.

3.2.29 ARTS AND SCIENCE COLLEGES

Vinayaka Missions Kirupananda Variyar Arts and Science College, A.A. Govt. Arts College, Bharathiyar Arts and Science College for Women, Attur. A.V.S. College of Science, Govt. Arts College for Women, Govt. Arts College, Jairam Arts and Science College, Salem Sowdeswari College, Sri Sarada College for Women, Sri Sarada College of Education, Vysya College, Salem.

3.2.30 CATERING AND HOTEL MANAGEMENT COLLEGES

Bharath Institute of Catering Technology and Hotel Management, Cenneys Institute of Hotel Management, Shevaroys Institute of Catering Technology and Hotel Management, Thiagarajar Institute of Catering Technology and Hotel Management, V.S.R. Catering and Hotel Management, Vinayaga Mission Arts and Science College, Salem.

3.2.31 DENTAL COLLEGES

Vinayaka Mission's Sankarachariyar Dental College, Salem.3.21.2

3.2.32 ENGINEERING COLLEGES

Sona College of Technology, Vinayaka Mission's Kirupanada Variyar Engineering College, Govt. Engineering College, Salem.

3.2.33 HOMOEOPATHY

Vinayaka Mission's Homoeopathic Medical College, Tamil Nadu Homoeopathy Medical College, Salem.

3.2.34 MANAGEMENT COLLEGES

Vinayaka Mission's Institute of Management, Sona School of Management, Vysya Institute of Management Studies, Salem.

3.2.35 MEDICAL COLLEGES

Vinayaka Mission's Kirupananda Variyar Medical College, Govt. Mohan Kumaramangalam Medical College, Salem.

3.2.36 NURSING COLLEGES

Vinayaka Mission's Annapoorna College of Nursing, Shanmuga College of Nursing, Sri Gokulam College of Nursing, Salem.

3.2.37 PHARMACY COLLEGES

Vinayaka Mission's College of Pharmacy, Salem

3.2.38 PHYSIOTHERAPY COLLEGES

Vinayaka Mission's College of Physiotherapy, Annai Therasa Institute of Paramedical Sciences, Gokulam Institute of Paramedical Sciences, Shanmugha College of Physiotherapy, Salem.

3.2.39 POLYTECHNIC COLLEGES

Thiagarajar Polytechnic College, Salem, C.S.I. Polytechnic College, Salem, D.P.C. Polytechnic College, Salem, Maruthi Polytechnic College, Salem, Murugesan Institute of Technology, Salem, Rajaji Institute of Technology, Salem, The Kavery Polytechnic College, Salem, The Salem Polytechnic College, Salem, Vinayaka Mission's Kirupananda Variyar Sundara Swamigal Polytechnic College, Salem.

3.2.40 TRANSPORT AND TRAFFIC

Three important National Highways (NH7, NH47 and NH68) criss-cross the city. Salem acts as the major transit point for Bangalore/ Coimbatore/ Madurai/ Chennai. This keeps the 6/4-lane bypass road of the city busy round the clock. The presence of the bypass road eases the congestion in the city roads as the mofussil buses bound for and from Namakkal, Coimbatore, Erode, Trichy, Madurai are diverted through the bypass road to enter the Central Bus Terminus.

The important arterial roads of the city are:

- Omalur Road (From Thiruvalluvar statue to Five roads and beyond)
- Sharadha College Road (From Five Roads to Hasthamppatty round-tana)
- Cherry Road (From Hasthampatty round-tana to Thiruvalluvar statue)
- Trichy Road (From Fort to Seelanaickenpatti and beyond)

- Yercaud Road (From Hasthampatty round-tana to Yercaud Foot Hills and
- Cuddalore Road (From Ammapet to Ayodhyapattinam and beyond)
- Peramanur Road (From Four roads to Peramanur)
- Ramakrishna Road
- Thammannan Road (From Four Roads to Leigh Bazaar)
- Junction Road (From Five Roads to Junction)
- Meyyanur Road (From Five Roads to Three Roads)
- The bypass road

3.3 SLUMS IN GLOBAL, NATIONAL AND INDIA

3.3.1 GLOBAL SLUM - AN OUTLOOK

In the 19th and early 20th century, slums were common in urban history of the United States and Europe. In the next century, slums are predominantly found in urban regions of developing and undeveloped parts of the world, but also found in developed economies. According to UN-Habitat, 32.7 percent of the urban population in the developing world in 2012 lived in slums. Global slum prevalence was highest in Sub-Saharan Africa (61.7 percent), followed by South Asia (35 percent), Southeast Asia (31 percent), East Asia (28.2 percent), West Asia (24.6 percent), Oceania (24.1 percent), Latin America and the Caribbean (23.5 percent), and North Africa (13.3 percent). Among individual countries, the proportion of urban residents living in slums in 2009 was highest in the Central African Republic (95.9 percent), Chad (89.3 percent), Niger (81.7 percent), and Mozambique (80.5 percent).

The five largest slums in the world are Neza-Chalco-Itza, Orangi, Dharavi, Khayelitsha and Kibera. One of Mexico City's many barrios, Neza-Chalco-Itza is the largest slum in the world with roughly four million people. Slums in Mexico City began growing in the early 1900s when the railroad brought new industry -- as well as new industrial zones -- to the city. As with many slums, most people in Neza-Chalco-Itza live illegally on unauthorized land. About 10 percent of all the residents of the Mexican capital live in these areas. Technically only 10 years old, the township in Karachi, Pakistan is home to 1.5 million people and still growing. Orangi, with 22 square miles of space, is significantly less dense than most urban slums and also more structured. After Orangi, the largest slum in Asia is

Dharavi in Mumbai. About one million people reside on just one square mile of space that was formerly a mangrove swamp. People became flocking to the area as the tanning and textile industries boomed and Dharavi's population density is now 11 times higher than that of the city that encompasses it. Khayelitsha is now the biggest of South Africa and the community had a population explosion after apartheid ended and blacks rushed into Cape Town for jobs. As of the last census in 2005, there were a recorded 400,000 people in Khayelitsha. A neighborhood in Nairobi, Kenya, the Kibera slum is the second largest in Africa, with anywhere from 200,000 to one million residents. Kibera is often used as the model for the environmental impact of informal settlement. However, Kibera is also one prototype for urban renewal and slum upgrading projects. Rounding out a list of the 10 biggest slums would include communities in Bogota, Colombia; Baghdad, Iraq, Venezuela, and Ghana. In the modern, global economy, urbanization is a trend that is impossible to buck and informal settlements are a necessary part of the process. Slum population in developed and developing countries, during 1990 to 2020.

Table 3.3 : Slum Population in Developed and Developing Countries (in 1000)

Major area, region, country or area	1990	2001	2005	2010	2015	2020
Developed Regions Europe	32,234 (4.47)	33,124 (3.58)	33,368 (3.29)	33,756 (2.95)	34,147 (2.63)	34,543 (2.34)
Other	18,723 (2.59)	20,934 (2.27)	21,903 (2.16)	23,079 (2.01)	24,318 (1.87)	25,623 (1.73)
Developing Regions Northern Africa	21,719 (3.01)	21,345 (2.31)	21,224 (2.09)	21,062 (1.84)	20,901 (1.61)	20,741 (1.40)
Sub-Saharan Africa	100,973 (13.99)	166,126 (17.98)	199,231 (19.62)	249,885 (21.81)	313,418 (24.14)	393,104 (26.61)
Latin America and the Caribbean	110,837 (15.36)	127,404 (13.79)	134,257 (13.22)	143,116 (12.49)	152,560 (11.75)	162,626 (11.01)
Eastern Asia	150,761 (20.89)	194,078 (21.00)	212,368(20.92)	238,061 (20.77)	266,863 (20.55)	299,150 (20.25)
South-central Asia	207,501 (28.76)	262,441 (28.40)	285,713(28.14)	317,858 (27.74)	353,620 (27.23)	393,405 (26.63)
South-eastern Asia	48,986 (6.79)	56,799 (6.15)	59,913(5.90)	64,073 (5.59)	68,521 (5.28)	73,279 (4.96)
Western Asia	29,524 (4.09)	41,356 (4.48)	46,709(4.60)	54,426 (4.75)	63,418 (4.88)	73,896 (5.00)
Oceania	350 (0.05)	499 (0.05)	568 (0.06)	668 (0.06)	786 (0.06)	924 (0.06)
Total	721,608 (100.00)	924,107 (100.00)	1,015,255 (100.00)	1,145,984 (100.00)	1,298,552 (100.00)	1,477,291 (100.00)

Source : UN-HABITAT (United Nations Population Division, World Urbanization Prospects, 2007)

The above table shows past, present and projected growth in the slum population around the world. Most of the slum population of the world will live in developing countries. In the year 2001, 94 per cent of the slum population of the world has been in the developing countries. The percentage will go up to 96 per cent in the year 2020 A.D. The percentage of highest concentration of slums is in South-Central Asia and Eastern Asia during 1990, which contributes nearly 50 per cent, whereas in 2020A.D it is from South-Central Asia and Sub-Saharan Africa accounts for 53 percent of slum population. Due to the implementation of various slum development programmes in developed regions the percentage of slums are gradually decreasing in nature.

3.3.2 INDIAN SCENARIO OF SLUM

In India, there has been an alarming increase in the slum population mostly due to the migration of the rural poor. It has been reported that the total slum population in India has doubled in the past two decades and has risen from 27.9 million in 1981 to 42.6 million in 2001. According to the 2001 Census, 640 cities and towns in India reported slums and the total slum population comprised 22.58 per cent of the total urban population of the states/union territories reporting slums. The financial capital of India known as Mumbai is home to estimate 6.5 million slum people. Nearly half of Mumbai's Population lives in small shacks surrounded by open sewers. Nearly 55per cent of Mumbai's population lives in Slum areas. After Mumbai, Delhi has the second largest slum Population in India. Nearly 1.8 million people lives in slum areas in capital of India - New Delhi. These people are mostly unemployed or daily wage workers who cannot even afford basic necessities of life.

The number of people living in slums in India has more than doubled in the past two decades and now exceeds the entire population of Britain, the Indian Government has announced. India has the highest concentration of slum dwellers in South Asia. 63 percent of the slum dwellers of Southern Asia, numbering about 170 million people are living in India.

Table 3.4 : Slum Population in India (2001-2011)

S. No	State/UT	Population			Male			Female		
		2001	2011	Percent Change	2001	2011	Percent Change	2001	2011	Percent Change
	India	42,578,150	65,494,604	53.82	22,697,218	33,968,203	49.66	19,880,932	31,526,401	58.58
1	Andaman & Nicobar Islands	16,244	14,172	-12.76	8,855	7,386	-16.59	7,389	6,786	-8.16
2	Andhra Pradesh	5,187,493	10,186,934	96.37	2,625,745	5,103,377	94.36	2,561,748	5,083,557	98.44
3	Arunachal Pradesh	0	15,562	0	0	8,029	0	0	7,533	0
4	Assam	82,289	197,266	139.72	43,472	101,424	133.31	38,817	95,842	146.91
5	Bihar	531,481	1,237,682	132.87	282,772	649,475	129.68	248,709	588,207	136.50
6	Chandigarh	107,125	95,135	-11.19	62,762	53,340	-15.01	44,363	41,795	-5.79
7	Chhatisgarh	817,908	1,898,931	132.17	422,096	966,623	129.00	395,812	932,308	135.54
8	Delhi	2,029,755	1,785,390	-12.04	1,140,334	974,329	-14.56	889,421	811,061	-8.81
9	Goa	14,482	26,247	81.24	7,469	13,826	85.11	7,013	12,421	77.11
10	Gujarat	1,866,797	1,680,095	-10.00	1,020,288	912,571	-10.56	846,509	767,524	-9.33
11	Haryana	1,420,407	1,662,305	17.03	778,734	887,947	14.02	641,673	774,358	20.68
12	Himachal Pradesh	0	61,312	0	0	32,555	0	0	28,757	0
13	Jammu & Kashmir	268,513	662,062	146.57	143,416	342,422	138.76	125,097	319,640	155.51
14	Jharkhand	301,569	372,999	23.69	158,532	192,908	21.68	143,037	180,091	25.91
15	Karnataka	1,402,971	3,291,434	134.60	714,413	1,650,724	131.06	688,558	1,640,710	138.28
16	Kerala	64,556	202,048	212.98	31,699	97,429	207.36	32,857	104,619	218.41

S. No	State/UT	Population			Male			Female		
		2001	2011	Percent Change	2001	2011	Percent Change	2001	2011	Percent Change
17	Madhya Pradesh	2,417,091	5,688,993	135.37	1,269,757	2,957,524	132.92	1,147,334	2,731,469	138.07
18	Maharashtra	11,202,762	11,848,423	5.76	6,137,624	6,328,217	3.11	5,065,138	5,520,206	8.98
19	Meghalaya	86,304	57,418	-33.47	43,078	28,737	-33.29	43,226	28,681	-33.65
20	Mizoram	0	78,561	0	0	38,861	0	0	39,700	0
21	Nagaland	0	82,324	0	0	42,651	0	0	39,673	0
22	Odisha	629,999	1,560,303	147.67	330,054	800,963	142.68	299,945	759,340	153.16
23	Puducherry	73,169	144,573	97.59	36,012	70,491	95.74	37,157	74,082	99.38
24	Punjab	1,159,561	1,460,518	25.95	629,326	776,388	23.37	530,235	684,130	29.02
25	Rajasthan	1,294,106	2,068,000	59.80	681,541	1,078,991	58.32	612,565	989,009	61.45
26	Sikkim	0	31,378	0	0	16,216	0	0	15,162	0
27	Tamil Nadu	2,866,893	5,798,459	102.26	1,441,437	2,886,993	100.29	1,425,456	2,911,466	104.25
28	Tripura	29,949	139,780	366.73	15,093	70,143	364.74	14,856	69,637	368.75
29	Uttar Pradesh	4,395,276	6,239,965	41.97	2,348,679	3,298,339	40.43	2,046,597	2,941,626	43.73
30	Uttarakhand	195,470	487,741	149.52	103,895	257,624	147.97	91,575	230,117	151.29
31	West Bengal	4,115,980	6,418,594	55.94	2,220,135	3,321,700	49.62	1,895,845	3,096,894	63.35

Source : Census of India, 2001 and 201

The above table reveals that in 2001, the slum population was around 43 million. A decade later in 2011, it was over 65 million calculation based on census reports shows that people lived in slums up by 53 percent in India. The growth of slum population by gender is also progressing. Male slum population is increasing from 22.7 million in 2001 to 34 million in 2011, whereas the same trend in case of females in 2001 to 32 million in 2011. The percent change in slum population during a decade is more than cent percent in 11 states in India, TamilNadu is one among the state.

With over 11 million of its residents in slums, Maharashtra has the highest slum population. Andhra Pradesh follows with over 10 million in slum and West Bengal and Uttar Pradesh have over 6 million slum residents each. These states are followed by TamilNadu and Madhya Pradesh has over 5 million slum residents each. The reason for the highest slum population in those states is that it includes million plus cities such as Mumbai, Kolkata, Delhi, Chennai, Hyderabad, Kanpur, Ahmedabad, Pune and Surat. Rapid industralisation along with in-migration is the factor that causes increasing slum population in that states. During 2001 census, 10 states are not reported as slum but in 2011 census Himachal Pradesh, Sikkim, Arunachal Pradesh, Nagaland and Mizhoram are reported as slum states. The least slum population is in Goa, Andaman and Nicobar Island and Tripura.

3.3.3 SLUM POPULATION IN TAMIL NADU

The total slum population of Tamil Nadu in the selected 63 Municipal Towns as per the Census of India 2001 is 2,838,366. This forms around 20.02 per cent of the total population of the selected Towns. The largest slum population is found in the Chennai Corporation where 10,79,414 persons are reported as slum dwellers. This forms 25.6 per cent of the total population. Madurai Corporation (1.76 lakhs/19 per cent), Tiruchirappalli Corporation (1.62 lakhs/22 per cent) and Salem Corporation (1.39 lakhs/20 per cent) are the other cities having more than one lakh slum dwellers.

The following table depicts district-wise slum population and number of literates with males and females in Tamil Nadu.

Table 3.5 : District - Wise Slum Population & Number of Literates in Tamil Nadu

District Name	Population			Literates		
	Total	Male	Female	Total	Male	Female
Ariyalur	16750	8282	8468	10788	5889	4899
Coimbatore	262033	130474	131559	189790	100970	88820
Cuddalore	145331	72091	73240	100158	54345	45813
Dharmapuri	48115	24159	23956	32231	17671	14560
Dindigal	169331	83615	85716	126344	66616	59728
Erode	168858	84190	84668	103916	57451	46465
Kancheepuram	1727402	862495	864907	1315643	692152	623491
Kanniyakumari	24390	12080	12310	19553	9899	9654
Karur	45923	22505	23418	32761	17600	15161
Krishnagiri	26053	12981	13072	17844	9614	8230
Madurai	337321	168677	168644	257064	136802	120262
Nagapattinam	104537	51490	53047	78512	41316	37196
Namakkal	42129	21109	21020	28298	15662	12636
Perambalur	15661	7808	7853	11875	6357	5518
Pudukkottai	113800	56066	57734	85890	45408	40482
Ramanathapuram	65002	32473	32529	48069	25627	22442
Salem	310831	157051	153780	207133	114451	92682
Sivagangai	83067	41532	41535	61353	32985	28368
Thanjavur	121507	59744	61763	90088	47391	42697
The Nilgiris	68385	33271	35114	51268	27020	24248
Theni	166768	83624	83144	113604	62537	51067
Thirunelveli	158771	77883	80888	114144	60994	53150
Thiruvallur	386800	193662	193138	295248	156372	138876
Thiruvannamalai	100950	49723	51227	70457	37872	32585
Thiruvarur	63571	31265	32306	47545	24958	22587
Thoothukkudi	78322	38905	39417	60730	31192	29538

District Name	Population			Literates		
	Total	Male	Female	Total	Male	Female
Tiruppur	131140	65789	65351	88861	48560	40301
Trichy	312729	154846	157883	239074	125833	113241
Vellore	224746	110405	114341	157806	83121	74685
Villupuram	108509	54332	54177	74220	40882	33338
Virudhunagar	169727	84466	85261	123451	66343	57108
TAMIL NADU	**5798459**	**2886993**	**2911466**	**4253718**	**2263890**	**1989828**

Source : Census of India 2011

The above table clearly explains that there are 5798459 slum dwellers in Tamil Nadu. Of 32 districts in Tamil Nadu, 7 districts are having more than state average of 181202 slum residents. Kancheepuram stands first in the total slum population (1727402) whereas the lowest numbers of persons (15661) are in Perambalur. Salem stands 5th place in the total number of slum population in Tamil Nadu (310831) and Thiruvallur stands second (386800), Madurai (337321) and Tirchy (312729) are in third and fourth places.

The total number of male slum population inTamilnadu is 2886993. Seven districts are having more than state average regarding male slum population. Kancheepuram stands first in male slum population (862495) whereas Perambalur has least number of male slum populations. Salem stands 4th place in male slum population. Regarding female slum population Tamil Nadu accounts for 2911466. This shows that female outnumbered male slum population in Tamil Nadu. Salem stands 5th place in female slum population and it shows that female is lower in number. The above districts are economically developing area and at the same time large numbers of people are in- migrants.

The number of slum literates in Tamil Nadu is 4253718 among that2263890 are male literates and remaining are female literates. In all the districts male literates are higher than female literates. Salem stands 5th place in number of literates whereas it is higher than state slum literates. Among the total districts only seven districts are having slum literates higher than state average.

Table 3.6 : Slum Population and Number of Literates in Tamil Nadu Municipal Corporation

Municipal Corporation	No of Household	Population			Literates		
		Persons	Males	Females	Persons	Males	Females
Chennai	329827	1342337	670176	672161	1021459	536570	484889
Madurai	72799	278153	139022	139131	215515	114014	101501
Tiruchirappalli	57225	228518	113528	114990	178756	93494	85262
Salem	46672	180936	91183	89753	124511	67853	56658
Coimbatore	34343	129181	64502	64679	95763	50728	45035
Tiruppur	19901	71856	36322	35534	51267	27808	23459
Tirunelveli	17344	68202	33266	34936	52083	27012	25071
Thoothukkudi	9836	39070	19412	19658	31116	15817	15299
Vellore	9689	42991	21102	21889	30096	15855	14241
Erode	7838	27572	13673	13899	19799	10646	9153

Source : Census of India, 2011

There are 10 municipal corporations in Tamil Nadu. The following table depicts Tamil Nadu municipal corporation's slum population and number of literates with gender. Chennai corporation has the highest slum population with over1 million followed by Madurai (2.8 lakhs), Thiruchirappali (2.3 Lakhs), Salem (1.8 Lakhs) and Coimbatore (1.3 Lakhs).

A look upon gender wise slum population in Chennai, Madurai, Tiruchirappali, Coimbatore, Tirunelvelli, Thoothukkudi and Vellore corporation female outnumbered male population. This shows that number of females residing are higher due to widowhood and more life expectancy of women in slum. In case of number of literates in municipal corporations more than 75 percent of its residents are literates. Male literates are higher in all corporations when compared to female literates.

3.3.4 STATUS OF SLUMS IN SALEM CITY

Table 3.7: Status of Slums in Salem City

	No. of Slums			**No. of Slum Households**		
NSS Round	**Notified**	**Non-Notified**	**Total**	**Notified**	**Non-Notified**	**Total**
NSS 417 (1993), 49th	20364	35947	56311	2606700	3327300	5934000
NSS 486 (2002), 58th	26166	25522	51688	5358272	2871472	8229744
NSS 534 (2009), 65th	24781	24213	48994	NA	NA	NA
NSS 561 (2012), 69th	13761	19749	33510	5559771	3249236	8809007
Salem Municipal Corporation	207	39	246	33512	5071	38583

Source : National Sample Survey Office (NSSO), NSS Report No: 417, 486, 534 & 561, Census of India, 2011

The NSSO surveys on slums conducted at various rounds presents decrease in the number of slums. However, it found an increase in the number of slum households. In India, the total numbers of urban slums were estimated at 56311, 51688, 48994 and 33510 in NSSO slum surveys conducted in 1993, 2002, 2009 and 2012 respectively. But, there was significant increase in the number of slum households from 5.9 million in 1993 to 8.8 million in 2012. According to 69th rounds survey on slums shows that 33510 slums existed in urban areas of India with 8.8 million households, in that 5.6 million households lived in notified slums and 3.2 million households in non-notified slums. According to Census of India

2011, in Salem Municipal Corporation totally 246 slums exists with 38583 slum households both in notified and non-notified slums.

3.3.5 TAMIL NADU SLUM CLEARANCE BOARD

Tamil Nadu Slum Clearance Board a pioneer institution for development and rehabilitation of urban slums was set up in 1970 for the clearance and improvement of urban slum areas in Tamil Nadu. It has been implementing various Housing, Slum Improvement and Rehabilitation and Resettlement schemes to ameliorate the living conditions of the slum dwellers in Tamil Nadu.

3.3.6 SLUM CLEARANCE AND UPGRADATION SCHEMES / PROGRAMMES

Urban governments are forced to face the challenges and issue of slum development in slum areas. The growing incidence of slums has thus resulted in new policies, programs and strategies by city authorities to improve the living conditions of slum dwellers. Governments have approached the problem with five main policy interventions according to UN-HABITAT (2008c). These policies started with slum clearance through violent forced evictions and large scale slum demolition. The second main intervention was the clearance and on-site redevelopment through self-help improving of existing infrastructure and facilities up to satisfactory standards. Later on, some policies were focused on the removal of slum residents from the central city to resettlement sites. The fourth intervention was the implementation of enabling policies focused on the integration of communities in the decision making processes. The last policy is slum upgrading which implemented participatory slum improvement interventions that integrated slum dwellers, government and agencies (World Bank 2008; UN-HABITAT 2003).

Indian government implementation of various possible financing schemes and development programme for improving housing conditions in slum communities play a pivotal role in urban areas. Among that a glimpse of few schemes were given below.

3.3.7 NATIONAL SLUM DEVELOPMENT PROGRAMME

The National Slum Development Programme (NSDP) was launched in August, 1996 at Kanpur in (U.P.) with the objective of up-gradation of urban slums. Under National Slum Development Programme, Additional Central Assistance (ACA) was being released to the States/UTs for the development of urban slums. The funds under NSDP was used for provision of physical infrastructure like water supply, storm water drains, community bath, widening and paving of existing lanes, sewers, community latrines, street lights and social amenities like preschool education, non-formal education adult education, maternity, child health and primary health care including immunization etc. The programme also had a component of shelter up gradation or construction of new houses. NSDP has since been discontinued from the financial year 2005-06. As reported by the States/ UTs, since the inception of the programme and upto 31-08-2006 out of the total funds of Rs.3089.63 crore released by the Central Government, an amount of Rs. 2496.18 crore has been spent and about 4.58 crores of slum dwellers have benefited from this programme.

3.3.8 VALMIKI AMBEDKAR AWAS YOJANA

Valmiki Ambedkar Awas Yojana (VAMBAY) launched on December 2001 was the first scheme exclusively for slum dwellers to facilitate the construction and upgradation of the dwelling units and to provide health and enabling urban environment through community toilets with a Government of India subsidy of 50 per cent; the balance 50 per cent to be arranged by the State Government. The State's share may consist of funds from any source in the form of subsidy or loan from Housing and Urban Development Corporation Limited (HUDCO) or any other agency. The funds are released by this Ministry only after a VAMBAY account is opened by the State Nodal Agency and the share of the State/Union Territory Government is deposited in that account.

3.3.9 INTEGRATED HOUSING AND SLUM DEVELOPMENT PROGRAMME (IHSDP)

Integrated Housing and Slum Development Programme aims at combining the existing schemes of VAMBAY and NSDP under this scheme. It is an integrated approach in ameliorating the conditions of the urban slum dwellers that do not possess adequate shatter and reside in dilapidated conditions. The scheme is applicable to all cities and towns as per 2001 census except cities/towns covered under Jawaharala Nehru Urban Renewal Mission (JNNURM). It enhances public and private investment in housing and infrastructure development in urban areas. The components for assistance under the scheme will include all slum improvement/ upgradation relocation projects including upgradation / new construction of houses and infrastructural facilities like water supply and sewerage. Cost of land for this project has to be born by the state Government. Title of the land should preferably be in the name of the wife and alternatively jointly in the names of husband and wife. In exceptional cases, title in the name of male beneficiary may be permitted. Ceiling cost for dwelling unit was Rs. 80,000 percent. Housing should not be provided free to the beneficiaries by the state government. A minimum o 12 percent beneficiary contribution should be stipulated, which in the case of SC/ST/BC/PH and other weaker sections shall be 10 percent. Minimum floor area of dwelling unit should not be less than 25 Square Meters and preferably two room accommodation plus kitchen and toilet should be constructed.

3.3.10 RAJIV AWAS YOJANA

In a bid to make the state slum-free, the Tamil Nadu government has selected nine urban agglomerations under the Rajiv Awas Yojana (RAY) for preparing proper rehabilitation plans. Nine cities including Chennai, Madurai, Coimbatore, Erode, Tiruppur, Tiruchy, Tirunelveli, Salem and Vellore come under the plan. RAY may be extended to all 25 urban agglomerations with more than 1,00,000 population based on the 2011 census and subsequently to all urban areas.

3.4 CONCLUSION

This chapter provides an overview of the status of slums at international, national, and regional levels. Slum dwellers have faced unique problems for long years, including poor health status, low living conditions, and limited educational opportunities. Many global and national programs have been established to directly address the living conditions of the urban poor. Consequently, there have been some improvements among slum dwellers through various welfare schemes in India.

Chapter IV

LIVING CONDITIONS OF URBAN SLUM AREA

4.1 INTRODUCTION

The present chapter deals with the socioeconomic status as well as living environmental conditions of slum dwellers. The first and foremost objective of this study is to incorporate the socioeconomic background of slum dwellers. Socioeconomic status (SES) is commonly conceptualized as the social standing or class of an individual or group. It is a measure of an individual's or family's economic and social position based on education, income and occupation. SES is a strong predictor of health, education and living environment of slum dwellers, without an assessment of it, the research would be incomplete. Therefore an attempt has been made in this chapter to study SES of slum dwellers such as age, sex, marital status, educational attainment, occupational status, monthly income, religion, caste, size and type of family, property and native place.

4.2 INDIVIDUAL CHARACTERISTICS OF SAMPLE HOUSEHOLDS

Table 4.1 depicts individual characteristics of sample household members in slums. In the sample households, the total number of household members were 1696. It was analysed with the help of age, sex, marital status, educational level, occupational status and individual earnings of members.

Table 4.1 : Individual Characteristics of Sample Households

Variables	Frequency	Percent
Age Group		
Less than 56-15	171	10.1
16-30	306	18.0
31-45	498	29.4
46-60	399	23.5
Above 60	234	13.8
	88	5.2
Sex		
Male	856	50.5
Female	840	49.5
Marital Status		
Never Married	713	42.0
Married	879	51.8
Widow / Divorced / Separated	14	6.2
Educational level		
Illiterate	480	28.3
Primary level	375	22.11
Middle level	310	18.28
Secondary level	278	16.39
Higher Secondary	97	5.72
College	156	9.20
Occupational Status		
Non-worker	959	56.54
Salaried people	169	9.96
Wage earners	447	26.36
Self employed	121	7.14
Individual Earnings		
Non- earning members	959	56.54
Less than 5000	376	22.16
5001-10000	272	16.0
10001-15000	73	4.3
Above 15000	16	1.0

Source : Primary Data

Age seems to be one of the major factors influencing labour force participation rate. It is the proportion of the population ages 15 and older that is economically active. More than two-third (71.90 per cent) of the slum dwellers were in productive age group above 15 years. Nearly 28 per cent were in unproductive age group less than 15 years. Around 29 per cent and 23 per cent fall under age categories of 16-30 years and 31-45 years. While more than one-tenth (13.8 per cent) lie under 46-60 age group. Remaining is aged more than 60 years.

A glimpse at the sex ratio shows that male outnumbered female only by one per cent. 50.50 per cent were male population and residual were female (49.50 per cent).

The marital status distribution depicts the social status of the respondents. The marital status is an important social variable, which creates some moral or financial support to the dependents. More than two-fifth (42 per cent) slum dwellers were unmarried and left over were married (58 per cent). Among married around 2 per cent were divorced / widow / separated.

Education generates specific cognitive, behavioural and social knowledge that are basic ingredients for the way of life. Though less than one third (28.3 per cent) slum dwellers was illiterate, more than 14 per cent had higher secondary and above. Around 20 per cent had primary education and 34.67 per cent of them had middle and secondary level education. Majority of them had primary education which helps them to read, write and calculate.

The occupational status is a fundamental indicator of economic soundness of households. Majority of slum dwellers were non-workers (56.54 per cent) which include students, housewife and others. It exhibits that more than 20 per cent were students. It can be observed that more than 40 per cent of the slum dwellers were engaged in various types of activities, mostly of unskilled works. The workers were classified into salaried persons, self employed and wage earners. Wage earners include construction workers, domestic servants, casual labourers, agricultural labourers and job works whereas salaried persons comprises of government employees and private employees such as mechanics, salesman, etc. Self employed consists of petty traders, vendors, recycling materials separators, etc. Around 26 per cent of the slum dwellers were daily wage workers, while one of every 8 slum dwellers were engaged in construction works.

Less than 10 per cent of slum dwellers were salaried workers and nearly 8 per cent of them were self employed.

Individual earnings facilitate to determine the economic status and dependency ratio of a household. More than half (56.54 per cent) of the household members were non-earning dependents and the rest were earning members. Among the total individual members, nearly one fifth of them were earning less than Rs.5000 per month, around 5 per cent were in above Rs.10001 income group and the left over 16 per cent of members were earning monthly income Rs.5001- Rs.10000.

Total dependency ratio was calculated among sample households and found that as 44.71 per cent. Among that child dependency ratio was 38.14 per cent and remaining were aged dependency ratio (6.57 per cent).

4.3 RELIGIOUS AND SOCIAL COMPOSITION

In social science research religion and social group plays a vital role. As the study is related to slum dwellers and their children education, their choice and preference to various activities are influenced by these social factors. The following table illustrates religious and social composition of slum respondents.

Table 4.2 : Religious and Social Composition

Variables	Frequency	Percent
Religion		
Hindu	310	77.50
Christian	41	10.30
Muslim	49	12.20
Social group		
Backward community	110	27.50
Most backward community	147	36.80
Schedule Caste / Schedule Tribe	143	35.70

Source : Primary Data

Religions of the respondents were mainly distributed as Hindu, Christian and Muslims. Around 75 per cent of the slum dwellers belonged to Hindu and the rest of the respondents belonged to Christian (10.20 per cent) and Muslims (12.20 per cent).

Caste is an important social factor which influences the participation and involvement in social activities. It helps the researcher to find out whether a particular social group concentrates in slum areas. Among the total sample households, around 35 per cent of the households hailed from Most Backward Class as well as Scheduled Caste/ Scheduled Tribes. Nearly 27 per cent of slum households represented the Backward Class. All social groups were included only in few slums (22 per cent) but in the remaining slums concentration of particular community was observed. Concentration of particular social group helps in community participation for upliftment of dwelling areas.

4.4 TYPE AND SIZE OF FAMILY

Type and size of family is one of the important factor determining consumption and expenditure of the household. The following table indicates the same.

Table 4.3 : Type and Size of Family

Variables	Frequency	Percent
Type of family		
Joint	120	30.00
Nuclear	280	70.00
Family size		
Less than 3	117	29.20
4-5	208	52.00
Above 5	75	18.80

Source : Primary Data

It is observed from the type of family that only 30 per cent of slum dwellers were attached with joint family system and the remaining were living as nuclear family. It reflects the trend of disintegrating nature of joint families and taking the shape of nuclear families. In order to avoid quarrel, clash and egoism with younger generation, the parents themselves encourage to form new family, after the marriage of a son in a family, which results in arise of two nuclear families in one household. The breakdown of joint family system resulted in slowly disappearing feature of old people taking care of young ones in providing nutritious food, better health and quality education.

Family size of the respondents indicates the total number of family members living together. The most dominant family size among the respondents were 4-5 members which alone constitute 52 per cent to the total, followed by the family size of less than 3 members (29.20 per cent). The number of respondents, who had the family size above 5 members constituted 18.80 per cent. The mean size of the family members was found 4 only.

4.5 HOUSEHOLD MONTHLY INCOME

The earnings of family members play a vital role in running day to day life of the slum dwellers. It was most reliable form of security and welfare measure available for every household. It was also used to examine the general wealth of the households.

Table 4.4 : Household Monthly Income

Income (Rs.)	Frequency	Percent
Less than Rs. 5000	53	13.20
Rs.5001-Rs.10000	131	32.80
Rs.10001-Rs.15000	138	34.50
Rs.15001-Rs.20000	50	12.50
Above Rs.20000	28	7.00

Source : Primary Data

Out of the total, 34.50 per cent of the households earned monthly income between Rs.10001-Rs.15000, while 32.80 per cent of the households were making income in the range of Rs.5001- Rs.10000 per month. 13.20 per cent were in lower income category of less than Rs.5000 and around 19 per cent were earning above Rs.15000. This shows that majority of the individuals engaged in different occupation contributes substantial amount to their family income.

4.6 MONTHLY SAVINGS

Saving leads to economic progress of an individual as well as country by way of investment. The extent of saving by slum dwellers mainly depends on their preferences for future over present consumption, their expectations of future income and to some extent of rate of interest. Around 20 per cent of slum dwellers save monthly and the left over were non-savers. During financial shocks, saving serves as a cache and helps the slum dwellers to avoid taking of unnecessary debt. High economic dependency among slum dwellers had led to difficulty in saving.

Monthly saving was categorized into less than Rs.100, Rs.101 – Rs.500, Rs.501 – Rs.1000 and above Rs.1000. Out of the total respondents, nearly 9 per cent of them save monthly between Rs.101 – Rs.500, while 4.80 per cent of the respondents were saving in the range of 0- Rs.100 and 4.2 per cent save more than Rs.501 per month.

4.7 OWNERSHIP OF PROPERTY

Owning a house is considered to be an important form of asset, especially for low income family. The majority of residents owned their house (84.75) and remaining inhabits for rent. Though many residents owned houses, but they did not possess the ownership of land on which these houses were built. When the respondents were asked about availability legal documents of the land, they were not able to provide it. It was observed from the study that more than 55 per cent of the slum dwellers reside in porumbok land or public land for many years. Only few inhabitants claimed ownership of land from the government and got patta.

Property usually refers to a legal designation of the ownership of land or house. Owning property shows economic soundness and wealth of slum households. More than three fourth of slum households does not possess any property in form of land or house. Nearly one fourth of slum households possess property in form of house site, cultivable land, house, jewel, etc.

A look at property value of slum households depicted that majority did not possess any assets (77.80 per cent), about 12 per cent of respondents were holding property value more than Rs.150000, the remaining was pursued by less than Rs.50000 (4.50 per cent), 3.20 per cent have property value range from Rs.50001 to Rs.100000 and 2.80 per cent owned property worth between Rs.100001 to Rs.150000.

4.8 NATIVE PLACE

In most cities slum dwellers were in fact migrants who come to city with an economic motive. But in the study area, most of slum dwellers were non migrants (85 per cent) and the left behind were migrants. Among migrants, 10 per cent of the respondents were migrants from different districts inside Tamil Nadu and the rest (5 per cent) were from other states. These migrants often stay in the nearby place with relatives mostly of undesirable public sites.

4.9 REASONS FOR MIGRATION

Reasons for migration among slum dwellers were exhibited into better job opportunity, better education, poverty, crazy for urban living and others. Of the total migrants, nearly 4 per cent migrants reported better employment opportunity as reason for it. It was followed by poverty (8 per cent), better education for their children (3 per cent) and only a few respondents stated as crazy for urban living (1 per cent).

4.10 DURATION OF STAY OF RESIDENTS IN SLUM AREAS

The length of stay of residents in the area plays an important role in the study. The slum dwellers were inhabited in these areas for long periods of time. While majority of respondents (37.20 per cent) were inhabited for 21 to 30 years, 21.80 per cent of them resides for 31 to 40 years, followed by less than 10 years (14.20 per cent), 11 to 20 years (13.20 per cent) and the remaining by more than 40 years (13.60 per cent). Tamil Nadu Slum Clearance Board is giving priority to the residents who stayed in particular areas for long duration, in the way of upliftment and providing new houses under various schemes.

4.11 LIVING ENVIRONMENT OF THE SLUM DWELLERS

Household cleanliness is of paramount importance to personal and environmental hygiene. Once households are clean, environmental vectors can easily be controlled. Hence the present study focused on the living environmental factors in slum households and areas.

Table 4.5 : Type of House and Facilities Available Within the House

Variables	Frequency	Percent
Type of house		
Pucca	57	14.20
Semipucca	219	54.80
Katcha	124	31.0
Number of rooms		
1	178	44.50
2	122	30.50
3	59	14.80
Above 3	41	10.20
Separate kitchen		
Yes	168	42.00
No	232	58.00
Drinking water		
In house	33	8.20
Street tap	266	66.50
Tank water	78	19.50
Others	23	5.80
Electricity		
Yes	368	92.00
No	32	8.00
Ventilation		
Yes	290	72.50
No	110	27.50
Mosquito Repellent	333	83.25
	67	16.75
Yes		
No		

Source : Primary Data

Type of housing was a good primary indicator of the living conditions of the slum dwellers. Based on the materials used for construction, the structures of houses were classified into three categories, namely, pucca, semipucca and katcha. Pucca houses refers to structure whose walls and roof are made of materials like cement, concrete, stones, stone blocks, over burnt bricks, tiles, timber, galvanized or corrugated iron sheets, asbestos sheets, etc. A house structures either the walls or the roof made of partly pucca and partly katcha materials are known as semipucca houses. Katcha houses consists of a structure whose walls and roof are made of materials such as unburnt bricks, bamboo, mud, grass, leaves, reeds or thatch, etc. Among the respondents, nearly 55 per cent had semi pucca houses, followed by katcha houses (31 per cent) and only 14 per cent of the slum households had pucca houses. These showed that there exist coexistence between type of house and ownership of land. Absence of owning a land made them to live in undesirable conditions.

Number of rooms provides an indication of the size of a dwelling. More than 40 per cent families live in one room houses and that single room is used as bed room, sitting room, dining room, kitchen and store as living room or common room. While 30.50 per cent of the respondents have two rooms, followed by three (14.80 per cent) and more than 3 rooms (10.20 per cent). Nearly 55 per cent of families have more than one room but the total floor area of a dwelling is very low.

As slum dwellers live in one or two rooms, the desire to have a separate kitchen is far behind their imagination. Nearly three fifth of the respondents does not have separate kitchen while the remaining two fifth have separate room for cooking. Those who have separate kitchen cook inside their house and others used open space along with their house or in the corner of living room itself.

Regarding drinking water facility there are different sources like in house connection, street tap or public tap, tank water and other sources like well water, buying purified water, fetching water from distance places, etc. Almost two third of the respondents were fetching water through street tap. The remaining one third of them were getting water from tank water (19.50 per cent), own tap (8.20 per cent) and other sources (5.80 per cent). Inadequate supply of water by local bodies made women and female children to spend a considerable amount of time in fetching water by waiting in long queue. It indirectly affected education of children and women labour force participation to a certain extent.

Electricity lights up slum dwelling and used as power for all electrical appliances in home. Nearly about all of the respondents (92 per cent) stated that they have electricity in their houses. Only 8 per cent of households did not have source of lighting ie. electricity connection.

Ventilation allows air to move throughout the room and creates comfortable living and healthy working environment in the slums. While 72.50 per cent of the respondent rooms have just one window mostly of small size and the rest (27.50 per cent) have no window in their small room. Absence of ventilation leads to unclean air, affect physical environment and health.

Slums are also breeding ground for mosquitoes due to its dirty unhygienic nature. Mosquito plays a role in spreading virus by its itchy bites in humans and can cause fever, body aches, low energy and head ache. Therefore an attempt has been made whether slum households use any devices such as mosquito coils, liquids etc to control it. 83.25 per cent of them use mosquito repellents and 16.75 per cent did not use anything to defense it.

Table 4.6 : Type of Structure of Houses Compare with NSS Data

Type of House	**NSS Rounds**				Primary Data
	49th Round	**58th Round**	**65th Round**	**69th Round**	
Pucca	30.9	47.6	56.9	59.6	54.8
Semipucca	33.7	34.5	29.3	25.0	31.0
Katcha	35.4	17.9	13.8	15.4	14.2
Total	100	100	100	100	100

Source : Primary Data & National Sample Survey Office (NSSO), NSS Report No: 417, 486, 534 & 561

The 69th round of NSSO survey shows that 59.6 per cent of slum households have pucca structure, followed by semipucca structure (25 per cent) and katcha structure (15.4 per cent). A noticeable change has been found in the type of structure of houses in slums between 1993 and 2012 different NSSO survey rounds in the country. The comparison of primary data with NSSO 69th round survey of slums shows more or less same level by type of structure of houses exists in Salem urban slums also.

Table 4.7 : Type of Ownership of Land Compare with NSS Data

Type of Ownership	NSS Rounds			Primary Data
	58th Round	65th Round	69th Round	
Public	64.7	60.7	56	55
Private	35.3	39.3	44	45
Total	100	100	100	100

Source : Primary Data & National Sample Survey Office (NSSO), NSS Report No: 486, 534 & 561

This table shows the distribution of slums by type of ownership of land on which the slums are located. The 69th NSSO survey round reflects that at all India level nearly 44 per cent of slums are seen to be situated on private land and the remaining 56 per cent of slums are situated on public land such as land owned local bodies, railways and other public land. The comparison with NSSO survey data by type of ownership of land to Salem, it shows that more or less same level of slums situated in public and private lands.

Table 4.8 : Percentage Distribution of Slum Households by Status of Electricity Connection Compare with NSS Data

Distribution	NSS Rounds			Primary Data
	58th Round	65th Round	69th Round	
Yes	86.9	85.5	86.8	92
No	13.1	14.5	13.2	8
Total	100	100	100	100

Source : Primary Data & National Sample Survey Office (NSSO), NSS Report No: 486, 534 & 561

With regard to electricity connections for household use was available for 92 per cent of the slum households in the study area. As per the 69th round NSSO survey 87 per cent of slum households had electricity connections for household use. Similarly at all India level with the help of NSSO surveys show that more level of electricity connections for household use exists in Salem District urban slums.

Table 4.9 : Percentage Distribution of Slum Households by Status of Street Light Connection Compare with NSS Data

Street Light	NSS Rounds			Primary Data
	58th Round	**65th Round**	**69th Round**	
Yes	74	75.4	73.9	90.6
No	26	24.6	26.1	9.4
Total	100	100	100	100

Source : Primary Data & National Sample Survey Office (NSSO), NSS Report No: 486, 534 & 561

According to NSSO 58th round (2002) survey outcome, 26 per cent had no access to street light connection. The same result was also found in 69th round NSSO survey. There was a much variation in the primary data results that nearly 91 per cent of slum households have street light connection.

Table 4.10 : Major Source of Drinking Water Available in Slum households Compare with NSS Data

Type of Source	**NSS Rounds**				Primary Data
	49th Round	**58th Round**	**65th Round**	**69th Round**	
Tap	64.8	77.7	77.8	71.4	74.7
Tube Well / Hand Pump	26.7	15.7	17.0	20.4	19.5
Others	8.5	6.6	5.2	8.2	5.8
Total	100	100	100	100	100

Source : Primary Data & National Sample Survey Office (NSSO), NSS Report No: 417, 486, 534 & 561

Comparisons at different years1993, 2002, 2009 and 2012 at all India level with primary data are shown in table. According to NSSO survey rounds, the major source of drinking water available to residents of slums were classified into tap, tube well / hand pump and others. At all India level 69th NSSO survey round (2012), taps were the major source of drinking water to nearly 71 per cent of slum households. The next major source was tube well / hand pump, which were 20 per cent followed by other sources (8.2 per cent) such as protected and unprotected well etc. Thus the distribution of drinking water in both notified and non-notified slums was tap water. The source of drinking water with more or less same percentage was found in the study area also.

4.12 FUEL USED FOR COOKING

Women spend more times in kitchen by doing household chores like cooking, cleaning vessels etc. So, it is necessary to highlight type of fuel used for cooking by slum dwellers.

It is observed that four type of fuel are used for cooking by slum households with multiple responses. More than 50 per cent of the respondents use LPG for cooking, 17 per cent make use of kerosene and stove for cooking, 12.20 per cent employ wood as fuel in hand made oven, 10.50 per cent use fire wood and LPG in this purpose, 6.5 per cent utilize both fire wood and kerosene, only one per cent use induction stove for cooking purpose and 1.50 per cent use both cylinder gas and kerosene for this purpose.

Table 4.11 : Fuel Used for Cooking

Cooking fuel	Frequency	Percent
Wood	49	12.20
Kerosene	68	17.00
Induction Stove	4	1.00
LPG	205	51.20
Wood and LPG	42	10.50
Wood and Kerosene	26	6.50
Kerosene and LPG	6	1.50

Source : Primary Data

It is noted that more than half per cent of the respondents use LPG, benefits by way of reduced cooking time, better health, preservation of forest reserves, etc. The time saved can be utilized for productive activities such as income generation and improving the living conditions of their families.

4.13 AVAILABILITY OF DURABLE GOODS

The availability of durable goods is used as an indicator of socio-economic level. There was substantial increase in household assets regarding possessing of durable goods.

Table 4.12 : Availability of Durable Goods

Durable Goods	Yes	No
Radio	46 (11.50)	354 (88.50)
Television	360 (90.00)	40 (10.00)
Electric Fan	359 (87.50)	41 (10.25)
Mobile Phone	303 (75.75)	97 (24.25)
Refrigerator	90 (22.50)	310 (77.50)
Bicycle	259 (64.75)	141 (35.25)
Grinder and Mixer	267 (66.75)	133 (33.25)
Motorcycle	205 (51.25)	195 (48.75)
Others	73 (18.25)	327 (81.75)

Source : Primary Data

Almost all the respondents possess any one of the durable goods listed above. 11.50 per cent have radio, 90 per cent possess television, 87.50 per cent own electric fan, 75.75 per cent hold mobile phone, 22.50 per cent acquire refrigerator, 64.75 per cent obtain bicycle, 66.75 per cent possess grinder/mixer, 51.25 per cent have motorcycle and 18.25 per cent of the households own other assets such as washing machine, cupboard, chair, coolers, cot, sewing machine, etc. The latest and most effective technology penetrated in slum was mobile phones. Supply of free durable goods such as mixie, grinder, electric fan, television by the present and past Government of TamilNadu under welfare scheme made slum dwellers to possess these durable goods.

4.14 SANITARY CONDITIONS IN SLUMS

Sanitary conditions include facilities such as drainage, toilet, and bathroom and garbage clearance. Drainage system plays an important role in removing household waste water and storm water either by connecting with subsurface or surface drainage canal outlets.

Table 4.13 : Sanitary Conditions in Slums

Sanitary Facilities	Frequency	Percent
Drainage system		
Open pucca	76	19.00
Open katcha	225	56.20
No drainage	99	24.80
Toilet		
Inhouse	109	27.20
Neighbour	20	5.00
Public toilet	186	46.50
Open space	85	21.20
Bathroom		
Yes	56	14.00
No	344	86.00
Garbage clearance		
Municipality	280	70.00
Own arrangements	32	8.00
No arrangements	88	22.00
Washing area		
Yes	168	42.00
No	232	58.00

Source : Primary Data

More than half of the drainage system existed in the slum households were open katcha (56.20 per cent) followed by open pucca (19 per cent) constructed of pucca materials such as cement, bricks, etc. Absence of drainage system was found in 24.80 per cent of slums. Underground covered pucca drainage system was totally absent in all the slums due to the progress of the scheme in Salem city as a whole. Improper drainage system forms a stagnant pool that affords breeding sites for disease vectors in slums.

Access to toilets is essential for the maintenance of good environment. Almost 46.50 per cent of households use public toilet and around one fourth of slum households have their own toilet facility. Nearly one fifth of them use open space for defecation purpose and only 5 per cent sharing toilets with their neighbourhoods. Access to public toilet required a fee from Rs.2 to Rs.5 per person and location was far away. Many slum dwellers reported that they felt ashamed to use public toilet due to unhygienic condition and inadequate water supply. Absence of toilet facilities also results in an unhealthy environment contaminated by human waste.

Bathing helps in maintenance of personal hygiene. About 86 per cent of slum households did not have bath room and nearly one seventh avail this facility. Absence of sufficient space made them to have temporary arrangement for bath room along their houses with thatched leaves or waste construction materials. Inadequate water supply in slums along with bathing shelters discourages people from regular cleaning of the body.

Garbage clearance also includes slum household waste collection as a part of the process of waste management. About 70 per cent of slum households have access to municipal corporation dustbin for garbage disposal. Nearly 22 per cent of them do not have any arrangement so dumped garbage in unused open place nearby their houses such as roadside, ditches, drain, etc. Rest of the respondents (8 per cent) made own arrangements for garbage collection.

Washing includes clothes cleaning process and drying. Availability of sufficient space for cleaning and drying clothes in slum houses were totally absent in 58 per cent of the households and they use little space in front of houses or streets for this purpose. More than two fifth of slum houses have sufficient space for washing clothes. Various environmental impacts arise during clothes cleaning processes like water pollution.

4.15 ROAD FACILITIES

Among basic infrastructure facilities, road plays a pivotal role in development of the city. In most slums, roads are motorable approach. About 55.30 per cent of slums had semi pucca road, followed by pucca (26.50 per cent) and katcha or absence of road (18.20 per cent) inside the slums.

4.16 STREET LIGHTS

Street lamps provides source of light for slum pedestrians on a road or walkway and increases their safety. More than 90 per cent of the slum households reported availability of stand lamps in their street and in the remaining cases absence of light sources in the streets.

4.17 POSSESSION OF VARIOUS IDENTITY CARDS

Ration card is a very useful identification document for slum households and helps to procure essential commodities at a subsidized rate. More than four fifth (88.25 per cent) of slum households had public distribution system (PDS) cards. Most of slum households were living below the poverty line, entitled to avail special subsidies under various cards distinction exists in the state. PDS cards indirectly helps in reducing food expenses.

Voter identity is also an identity proof for casting vote and also serves as general purpose such as identity, address and age proof. Almost 96.25 per cent of the slum households possessed voter card. Slums were considered as voters bank most of them at eligible age hold this card. Free health insurance scheme was introduced by Government of Tamilnadu for the poorest of the poor/ low income / unorganized group who cannot afford costly treatment, as a supplementary facility for getting free treatment in empanelled government and private hospitals for some serious ailments. Nearly three fourth of the slum dwellers availed health insurance card and the remaining one fourth did not have such card.

Self help groups (SHGs) play a predominant role in empowerment of women in social, political and economic status. Nearly 62 per cent of the slum dwellers have been members of SHGs.

4.18 LIVING ENVIRONMENT INDEX (LEI)

Based on the facilities available in and around the households, the researcher constructed an index to study living environment of the sample households which is known as Living Environment Index. National Family Health Survey (NFHS) created a standard of living index as a summary of household measure which composed of 27 items, including consumer durables, agricultural machinery, housing conditions and access to basic services (IIPS 2000). Keeping the above method as a base, the researcher constructed an alternative method LEI by including and excluding some variables from it. The variables used and weightage assigned to particular variables to construct LEI were indicated in the table.

Table 4.14 : Living Environment Index (LEI) of slum households

Variables	Weightage Value
1. Type of house	Pucca – 2
	Semi- pucca - 1
	Katcha – 0
2. Availability of separate kitchen	Yes – 1
	No – 0
3. Location of drinking water	Inhouse – 3
	Public tap – 2
	Tank water – 1
	Others – 0
4. Number of rooms	More than 3 – 4
	Three rooms -3
	Two rooms – 2
	One room – 1
5. Availability of toilet	Inhouse – 2
	Public toilet – 1
	Open place – 0
6. Drainage connectivity	Pucca – 2
	Katcha – 1
	No drainage – 0
7. Garbage clearance	Municipality – 2
	Own arrangements -1
	Others – 0
8. Road facility	Pucca – 2
	Semi- pucca - 1
	Katcha – 0
9. Fuel used for cooking	LPG – 2
	Kerosene – 1
	Wood – 0
10. Availability of power connection	Electricity – 1
	Others – 0
11. Bathing facility	Yes – 1
	No – 0
12. Availability of ventilation	Yes – 1
	No – 0

Variables	Weightage Value
13. Washing facility	Yes – 1 No – 0
14. Street Light	Yes – 1 No – 0
15. Ownership of House	Owned – 2 Rented
Classification of Living Environment Index (LEI)	**Score Range**
Low	Below 15
Medium	15 – 18
High	Above 19

Source : Primary data

The LEI score has been derived by summing up the total of all the variables and its score ranges from 8 to 23. The researcher has classified the LEI into Low LEI, Medium LEI and High LEI based on the mean value (16.82) of LEI scores. As per the classification of LEI, most of the households were in low LEI (45 per cent) followed by medium LEI (37 per cent) and the remaining were in high LEI. Low LEI indicated that these slum dwellers were deprived of access to basic services such as water, fuel, sanitation, etc. Moreover all the slum household head were working but were engaged in low paid jobs. With this meager income it was difficult for them to improve their living environment.

4.19 CONCLUSION

In this chapter, the researcher explored the socio-economic background of the sample households. In socio-economic conditions, it covers various aspects such as individual characteristics of sample households, religious and social composition, type and size of family, monthly household income and savings, reasons for migration, ownership of property, duration of stay in slums, possession of various identity cards, fuel used for cooking, type of house, facilities available within house, availability of durable goods, sanitary conditions, street lights, road facilities and living environment index. In this prevailing environmental setup and socio-economic background, it is necessary to know about the education level and health conditions of the slum children in the study area. It is analysed in the forthcoming chapters.

Chapter V

EDUCATION OF SLUM CHILDRENS

5.1 INTRODUCTION

Education is a fundamental component of human capital, and a population's education level is a fundamental component of development. It is for the welfare and progress of people and its development is ultimately aimed at maximizing the capacity to fulfill the needs and requirement of the nation. Education has long been seen as an effective and powerful means for achieving economic growth, reducing poverty, improving individuals' earning potential and empowerment, promoting healthy populations, and building competitive economies (Hanushek and Wossman 2007; UNESCO 2007; World Bank 2006). Universal children's schooling is considered so important that World Bank included it as one of the Millennium Development Goals. School enrollment of developing world children has been studied by both academics and policy practitioners interested in increasing enrollment as both a means and an end of development.

In India since Independence (1947) several initiatives have been taken for qualitative and quantitative expansion of elementary education like operation black-board, District Primary Education Programme (DPEP), Sarva Shiksha Abhiyan (SSA), mid-day meal scheme and many others, one of the latest being RTE. The existences of the Right of Children to Free and Compulsory Education (RTE) Act 2009 marks a historic moment for the children of India. This Act serves as a building block to ensure that every child has his or her right (as an entitlement) to get a quality elementary education, and that the State, with the help of families and communities, fulfils this obligation. RTE provides a ripe platform to reach the unreached, with specific provisions for disadvantaged groups, such as child labourers, migrant children, children with special needs, or those who have a "disadvantage owing to social, cultural economical, geographical, linguistic, gender or such other factor". It provides a justifiable legal framework that entitles all children between the ages of 6 and 14 shall have the right to free and compulsory elementary education of reasonable quality, based on the principles of equity and non-discrimination at a neighborhood school. There is no direct (school fees) or indirect cost (uniforms, textbooks, mid-day meals, transportation) to be borne by the child or the parents to obtain elementary education. The government will provide schooling free-of-cost until a child's elementary education is completed.

5.2 IMPORTANCE OF SLUM CHILDREN EDUCATION

Education is considered both socially and personally an indispensible part of human life. It makes children in slum more ambitious, self confident and shapes their career. It helps them to earn respect and recognition in the society. It plays an active role in laying proper foundation for the over-all socio-economic development of slum dwellers. It leads to broad social benefits to individuals and improves the quality of their lives and society. It also helps slum dwellers to promote healthy surroundings, earn money, economic growth, rights for women and children in the society and betterment of mankind. Besides these, education is also acting as a fundamental agency to promote the capacity of slum dwellers to escape from poverty and hunger with their own power. Providing right type of education to slum children at right time is the key to slum development and human resource formation.

5.3 PATTERN OF EDUCATION

The education system in Salem District is based on the National and State level pattern which uniformly follows the "10+2+3" pattern of education. In this pattern, children study for 12 years in schools and then 3 years of undergraduate education for a bachelor's degree. The entry age in class 1 is 5+ whereas pre-primary classes form age group 3-5 years. School education consists of eight years of elementary education, that is, five years of primary (6-11 years) and three years of middle school education (11-14 years) respectively. It is followed by secondary (14-16 years) and higher secondary education (16-18 years) of two years each. The final two years of secondary is often called senior secondary or simply the "+2" stage. The two halves of secondary education are each an important stage, because to pursue higher education one need a pass certificate issued by Central Board of Education under Ministry of Human Resource Development.

Standing at this juncture it is absolutely necessary to understand and evaluate the present scenario of slum children education. Many studies have focused on slum children education from 6-14 years age. As government made elementary education compulsory for all, it is also possible for slum children to get education up to 14 years. So the present study covered the slum children school education from 6-18 years of age. Therefore an attempt has been made by the researcher to study the prevalent problems of non-enrolment i.e. drop-out, irregular attendance and access to school of slum children.

5.4 EDUCATION STATUS OF SLUM CHILDREN

A household affords a child with opportunities to develop into a stable and independent person, especially, through enabling the child to attend school. Education status of slum children comprises of enrolment and dropout. Enrolment refers to whether a child is currently enrolling any education institution. Those who are not currently attending school were called as dropout. Out of 400 households, it was observed that 620 children of age group 6-18 years in sample household.

Table 5.1 : Education Status of Slum Children with Education-Sex Matrix

Education Level	Male			Female			Total
	Enrolled	Dropout	Total	Enrolled	Dropout	Total	
Primary	95 (27.00)	_	95 (25.25)	49 (23.50)	1 (2.90)	50 (20.50)	**145** **(23.40)**
Middle	68 (19.40)	6 (24.00)	74 (19.70)	38 (18.20)	7 (20.00)	45 (18.50)	**119** **(19.20)**
Secondary	80 (22.80)	14 (56.00)	85 (22.60)	54 (25.80)	18 (51.40)	63 (25.80)	**148** **(23.90)**
Higher Secondary	108 (30.80)	5 (20.00)	122 (32.45)	68 (32.50)	9 (25.70)	86 (35.20)	**208** **(33.50)**
Total	**351** **(93.35)**	**25** **(6.65)**	**376** **(100)**	**209** **(85.65)**	**35** **(14.35)**	**244** **(100)**	**620** **(100)**

Source : Primary Data

Out of 620 children, 376 were male children and the remaining 244 were female children. Among male children, 93.35 per cent were enrolled in schools and remaining 6.65 per cent were dropout from schools. Out of total female children, 85.65 per cent were enrolled in different school levels and remaining 14.35 per cent were dropped out. 33.50 per cent were enrolled in higher secondary level, followed by secondary level (23.90 per cent), primary level (23.40 per cent) and middle level (19.20 per cent). Dropout was higher in secondary school level both in case of male (56 per cent) and female children (51.40 per cent). The reason for dropout at primary level was due to child ill health of cardiovascular disease. Disinterest of children and poor result in school is the major reason for dropout at secondary level. After the implementation of Mid-Day Meal schemes and Sarva Shiksha Abhiyan (SSA) enrolment of slum children in education stream showed a gradual increase.

5.5 TYPE OF SCHOOL

There exist different types of school in the study area such as government, aided and private. Government schools are referred to schools fully run, owned and managed by central, state or local governments. Aided schools are owned by private management but funded largely by government grant-in-aid. The rules and regulations followed in these schools are same as that of public schools and controlled by the concerned state government. It is also known as private aided or government aided or aided schools. Private schools are fully owned and controlled by the private management, but subject to government rules to some extent. These schools run entirely on fee-revenues and without state aid are also known as private unaided schools. Although aided and private education institutions are owned by the private management, their work nature, curriculum, etc. differ in many aspects. The table shows enrolment of children in different type of school.

The enrolment of slum children in government school alone made up 65.20 per cent of all school enrolment. More than one fourth of children were enrolled in aided school (30 per cent) and remaining in private schools (4.80 per cent). Among total respondents, 90.30 per cent were enrolled in different type of schools and nearly one tenth (9.70 per cent) were dropped out from schools. Dropout was higher in government schools (56.70 per cent) and followed by aided schools (43.30 per cent).

Table 5.2 : Type of school

Type of school	No. of children		Total (Percent)
	Enrolled	Dropout	
Government	370 (66.00)	34 (56.70)	**404 (65.20)**
Aided	160 (28.60)	26 (43.30)	**186 (30.00)**
Private	30 (5.40)	-	**30 (4.80)**
Total	**560 (90.30)**	**60 (9.70)**	**620 (100)**

Source : Primary data

Provision of mid-day meals along with various government welfare schemes in the school education resulted in higher enrolment of children in government schools. The parents who aspire for better education compared to government schools enroll their children in nearby aided schools. Some parents' sign up their children in private school was due to English medium instruction, school facilities and teacher attendance. The de facto privatisation of education reflects the growing number of private schools and the increasing number of student enrolment there has become prominent in urban slums also. As cost of education in private schools such as CBSE, ICSE, Anglo-Indian and International schools are comparatively higher to other private matriculation schools, none of the slum children was enrolled in these schools due to their financial position.

From the chi-square analysis on parental education and type of school, that the 'p' value is less than 0.05 (0.042) the null hypothesis is rejected at 10 percent level of significance. Hence it is concluded that there is a significant association between the parental education and types of school.

Table 5.3 : Cross Tabulation of Parental Education and Children Type of School

Parental Education	Type of School (Children)			Total (%)
	Government (%)	Aided school (%)	Private school (%)	
Illiterate	69 (18.70)	15 (9.40)	–	84 (15.00)
Primary level	75 (20.30)	21 (13.10)	–	96 (17.20)
Middle level	106 (28.60)	24 (15.00)	–	130 (23.20)
Secondary level	51 (13.80)	29 (18.10)	4 (13.30)	84 (15.00)
Higher Secondary	34 (9.20)	34 (21.30)	6 (20.00)	74 (13.20)
College	35 (9.40)	37 (23.10)	20 (66.70))	92 (16.40)
Total	**370(66.00)**	**160(28.60)**	**30(5.40)**	**560(100)**
Chi-square		**22.61**		
df		**13**		
P value		**0.042***		

Source : Computed from Primary Data

Note : Figures in Parentheses are Percentages to the column Total

**denote at p value ≥ 0.05, significance at 10 percent*

The educational attainment of the parents influences significantly on the students' enrollment in types of school. Parents who had not even entered into the school enrolled their siblings in government and aided schools. Parents who have completed degree enrolled their children in different type of schools but higher in case of private schools. Parents educated at primary and middle level made their children to enroll in government and aided schools. It was found that maximum number of years parents spent on education made their children to enroll in private schools. It may be due to rationale of awareness about the availability of infrastructure facilities and teacher-students ratio.

5.6 TYPE OF SCHOOL AND HOUSEHOLD MONTHLY INCOME

Enrolment of children in different stream of school is closely related with monthly income of households. School type along with income categories determines kind of financial assistance they can get for their siblings. The number of children enrolled in various types of schools at various income categories was presented below.

Table 5.4 : Type of school and Monthly Income of Households

Monthly Income	Types of School			Total
	Government school	Aided school	Private school	
Less than Rs. 5000	**150(40.60)**	26(16.20)	-	176(31.40)
Rs.5001-Rs.10000	**78(21.00)**	22(13.80)	3(10.00)	103(18.40)
Rs.10001-Rs.15000	60(16.20)	37(23.10)	**9(30.00)**	106(18.90)
Rs.15001-Rs.20000	45(12.20)	33(20.60)	**7(23.30)**	85(15.20)
Above Rs.20000	37(10.00)	42(26.30)	**11(36.70)**	90(16.10)
Total	**370(66.00)**	**160(28.60)**	**30(5.40)**	**560(100)**

Source : Primary data

Around forty per cent of children in income group less than Rs.5000 were attending government schools. Among income category Rs.5001 to Rs.10000, 21 per cent of children were more likely to attend government schools than government aided schools (13.80 per cent) and private schools (10 per cent). Private schools (30 per cent) were more catering for the need of income categories Rs.10001- Rs.15000. It was found that family monthly income above Rs.15000 particularly sends their children to government aided schools and private schools. As monthly income increases the enrolment of children in government aided and private schools showed a gradual progress. The location of government schools in and around slum areas does not mean that children in slum can attend only those schools.

To find out the significance between monthly income of households and types of school one way ANOVA was used.

ANALYSIS OF VARIANCE (ONE-WAY ANOVA)

Table 5.4(a) : ANOVA Significant Between Monthly Income Respects to Types of School

Types of School	Mean	S.D	F Value	P Value
Government school	20.00	2.05		
Aided school	17.00	3.14	7.152	**0.007***
Private school	21.00	3.18		

Source : Computed from Primary Data

*Note : *denote significant at 1 % level*

Ho= There is no significant different between monthly income and types of school.

Since p value is less than 0.01 the null hypothesis is rejected at 1% level of significant. Hence conclude that there is significant different between monthly income and types of school.

Monthly income of households plays a significant role in determining types of school. When a household earns more income, they enroll their children in private schools. If income level is lower, the household income allocation is mostly for fulfilling basic necessaries of life. So they are not able to allocate more proportion of income for education purpose. This makes household with low income to enroll their children in government and aided schools.

5.7 PURPOSE FOR SENDING SCHOOL

Initial schooling focus is generally around developing basic interpersonal communication and literacy skills in order to further ability to learn more complex skills and subjects. The purpose of education indeed any form that the transmission of knowledge, values, beliefs, skills, attitudes and habits from one generation to the next through schooling. It widely include to develop the intellect, to create an effective work force, to prepare students for a job or career, to serve social needs, to contribute to the economy and to promote a particular social or political system. The purpose for pursuing education can vary from individual to individual.

Table 5.5 : Purpose for Sending School

Purpose for sending school	No. of children's	Per cent
Better employment	98	17.50
Learn English	47	8.40
Needed in life	65	11.60
Better marriage	78	13.90
Earn respect	52	9.30
Free food	80	14.30
All these	140	25.00
Total	560	100

Source : Primary data

About one fifth children were sent to school to get better employment opportunities in the future, nearly 14.30 per cent children parents stated provision of free mid-day meals schemes was also an indirect reason for school enrolment, 11.60 per cent sign up their children in schools as it is basic need of day-to-day life, 8.40 per cent of parents intention was to learn English, whereas others reported better marriage (13.90 per cent) and to earn respect (9.30 per cent) were purposes of school sending. Nearly one fourth of parents (25 per cent) sent their child to school for all the above mentioned purposes.

5.8 ATTENDANCE BEHAVIOUR OF CHILDREN

Child's attendance is the biggest factor influencing their academic success. Children who attend school regularly are more likely to build good academic records, participate in the school community, learn valuable social skills and develop a broader world view. Regular attendance keeps the child disciplined, well versed with the curriculum and continuity in studies.

Table 5.6 : Regularly Attending School

Particulars	No. of Children's	Percent
Yes	515	92
No	45	8
Total	**560**	**100**

Source : Primary data

Out of the total children, 92 per cent of them were regularly attending the schools and 8 per cent of children were not attending the schools regularly.

5.9 REASONS FOR IRREGULAR ATTENDANCE

A student may be absent from their educational program from time to time. A child who did not attend school regularly have a difficult time passing their courses, lose track of the school syllabus, lower participation grades, catching up to their peers and poor performance on tests. A reason for child's absence may be sickness, poor performance, insufficient coaching, migration and lack of motivation of parents. The reason for irregular attendance is depicted in below table.

Table 5.7 : Reason for Not Regular Attendance (Irregular)

Reasons	No. of Children's	Percent
Sickness	12	26.60
Poor Performance	9	20.00
Insufficient Coaching	5	11.10
Migration of Parents	8	17.80
Distance of School	3	6.70
Lack of Motivation of the Parents	4	8.90
Others	4	8.90
Total	**45**	**100**

Source : Primary data

26.60 per cent of children were absent due to their sickness, more than one tenth were not interested in attending school due to insufficient coaching, less than one tenth stated lack of parents motivation to attend school regularly, one fifth of the absentees were poor performer in class and 17.80 per cent reported that children had gone to their native place. Absence of a child due to sickness is related to the poor living environment and sanitary conditions in which they stay. As children wander in and around these areas leading to various diseases resulted in low attendance in the schools.

5.10 REASONS FOR NON-ENROLMENT (DROP OUT)

Drop out was the major reasons for non-enrolment. Drop out refers to as the proportion of children who stop attending without terminating enrollment in the schooling system. The reasons for discontinuing school can be of personal, family and school related reasons which include low socio-economic status, low parental education, financial issues, employment of children, disinterest in school and school work, poor grades, poor health, poverty, other extenuating circumstances like marriage etc.

Table 5.8 : Reasons for Non-Enrolment (Drop out)

Reasons for non enrolment	No of children	Per cent
Disinterest	11	18.33
Financial problem	24	40.00
Employment	18	30.00
Poor result	4	6.67
Childs own long illness	1	3.33
Sickness of parents	2	1.67
Total	**60**	**100**

Source : Primary data

Two fifth of the children were forced to leave school due to family crisis i.e. financial crisis or poverty, less than one fifth were out of school due to lack of interest in their studies, almost one third dropped out as they started work to support their family, 6.67 per cent students inability to pass an examination led to reduction in the motivation level and they ultimately withdraw from school and 1.67 per cent of children had to leave the studies because their mother had fallen sick and they had to take care of younger siblings and household work. Around 3.33 per cent of children never attended the school due to acute health syndrome.

5.11 POSITION OF NON-ENROLLED (DROP OUT) CHILDREN

To study the position of non-enrolled (drop out) children is necessary, because they are adding anything to economic conditions of their family.

Table 5.9 : Position of Non-Enrolled (Drop out) Children

Position	No. of Children	Percent
Doing nothing	33	55.00
Helping their parents	7	11.70
Learning skills	12	20.00
Working	8	13.30
Total	**60**	**100**

Source : Primary data

Among children who dropped out, nearly half of children were 'doing nothing' at present, 20 per cent were learning skills such as carpentry, electrician related work, tailoring, embroidery and beautician courses, more than one fifth of them were employed and 11.70 per cent stay back in home or helping their parents in household activities.

5.12 EARNINGS OF NON-ENROLLED CHILDREN

The average earnings of the employed children were Rs. 3278 per month. As they were employed in unskilled or semi-skilled work in unorganised sector often restricted with lower pay and were trapped in dead end jobs owing to existence of skills gap and diminished networking opportunities with industry leaders and likeminded persons. The job market has grown extremely competitive therefore the economic effects of dropping out of schools are more severe to slum dwellers. Parents reported that employed children spent most of the amount by themselves rather than contributing to the household income. Dropping out consequences have long term above said economic and social repercussions.

5.13 DISTANCE OF THE SCHOOL

Home-to-school distance is the transporting of children to and from schools. This distance can be undertaken by school students themselves or they may be accompanied by family members or care givers, or the transport may be organized collectively using auto, vans or buses. It is identified as the strongest motive to active school participation or enrolment of slum children. A better understanding of the threshold of walkable distance will inform school planning and development. As per the Right of Children to Free and Compulsory Education Act 2009 access for primary school and upper primary school in respect of children, a school shall be to be established within a walking distance of 1 km and 3 km in the neighbourhood. According to Rashtriya Madhyamik Shiksha Abhiyan access to a secondary school and higher secondary school which to be provided within a reasonable distance of 5 kilometer and 7-10 kilometers of every habitation.

Table 5.10 : Distance of the School

Distance (in kms.)	No. of Children	Per cent
Less than 1	140	25.00
1-3	340	60.70
Above 3	80	14.30
Total	560	100

Source : Primary data

Based on the length, distance of the school is classified into less than 1 km, between 1 to 3 kms and above 3 kms. To reach school, three fifth of children have to journey between 1-3 kms distance whereas one fourth of kids have to travel within 1 km from their habitat or residence. The rest of children (14.30 per cent) have to pass through distance more than 3 kms from school to their dwellings. This shows the availability of schools at reachable distance throughout the country after the implementation of SSA. Primary schools were accessible nearby slums, but middle and secondary schools being not available in the close vicinity children have to travel more than one kilometer.

Table 5.11 : Distribution of Slum Households by Distance from Primary School Compare with NSS Data

Distance (in km)	NSS Rounds				Primary Data
	49th Round	58th Round	65th Round	69th Round	
Less than 0.5	62.4	67.8	52.9	59.3	60.7
0.5 – 1	27.6	24.2	33.7	28.4	26.2
1 - 2	7.1	6.5	10.9	10.3	11.1
2 – 5	2.5	1.5	2.2	2.0	2.0
5 and above	0.4	0	0.3	0	0
Total	100	100	100	100	100

Source : Primary Data

National Sample Survey Office (NSSO), NSS Report No: 417, 486, 534 & 561

According to NSSO survey results, in 1993 round around 90 per cent of slum households had primary schools within 1 km distance and the percentage increased in 2002 by 92 per cent and slightly decreased to 87 per cent in 2009. But for 7 per cent of slum households nearest primary school was available within 1 to 2 km in 1993 and 2002; this has increased to 11 per cent in 2009. Exactly 2 per cent of slum households have primary school 2 to 5 km away in 1993 and 2002. In 69th round (2012) it is seen that for 59.3 per cent of slum households primary school was within less than 0.5 km distance whereas 28.4 per cent between 0.5 to 1 km, 10.3 per cent between 1 to 2 km and only in 2 per cent of slum households have accessibility to primary school was 2 to 5 km. comparison with 2012 round of NSSO survey with primary data shows more or less the same distance to primary schools.

5.14 MODE OF TRANSPORT

It is necessary to look at mode of transport used by the children in continuance with the distance of the school. Thus the mode of transport used by children to reach the school is depicted in the following table.

It was found that 32.10 per cent of children were deemed to be within walkable distance to school, so to cover the distance either they walked or used bicycles. While 37.50 per cent of children used local bus and more than one tenth (13.40 per cent) arranged for other means of transport such as auto rickshaws or private van and 17 per cent used parental transport such as two-wheeler to reach the school.

Table 5.12: Mode of transport on School Going Children

Type of Transport	No. of Children	Percent
Walk	180	**32.10**
Government Bus	210	**37.50**
Auto/Private Van	75	**13.40**
Parents drop by vehicle	95	**17.00**
Total	**560**	**100**

Source : Primary data

The most common mode of transport used by children was bus due to provision of free bus pass by the Ministry of Education. Parents commented that buses were overcrowded and insufficient in numbers during peak hours especially in areas with less transport frequency. Some children were to pass through more dangerous traffic conditions, circuitous routes while walking to school.

5.15 ANNUAL EXPENDITURE ON SCHOOL EDUCATION

Households incur expenditure on education irrespective of whether their child goes to a public school or a private school. The financial aspect of schooling i.e. the expenditure on schooling is a major determinant of the likelihood of the child going to school. The academic expenses incurred by the parents for a school going child can be categorized into expenditure on tuition fee, books, stationary, uniform, private coaching, transport and other academic expenditure.

Tuition fee refers to a fee charged by educational institutions to assist with funding a staff and faculty, course offerings, lab equipments, computer systems, libraries, facility upkeep and to provide a comfortable student learning environment. It changes at different rates from one type of institution to the next. 66 per cent of children were not incurring any tuition fee. More than one fourth of parents remitted less than Rs.500 as tuition fee. The rest of them paid more than Rs.500 as tuition fee for their children education. According to RTE Act 2009, no child shall be liable to pay any kind of fee or charges or expenses which may prevent him or her from pursuing and completing elementary education in a neighbourhood government school. Parents who enrolled the children in private institutions paid more tuition fee compared to other schools.

Table 5.13 : Annual Expenditure on School Education

Various Fees	Tuition Fees	Books, Stationary etc.,	Uniform Cost	Private Tuition	Transport Cost
Level of Expenses					
Nil	**370(66.00)**	-	**380(67.90)**	**200(35.70)**	**385(68.70)**
Less than 500	142(25.40)	**465(83.00)**	112(20.00)	180(32.10)	10(1.80)
501-1000	12(2.10)	38(6.80)	32(5.70)	120(21.50)	75(13.40)

Various Fees	Tuition Fees	Books, Stationary etc.,	Uniform Cost	Private Tuition	Transport Cost
Level of Expenses					
1001-1500	6(1.10)	15(2.70)	8(1.40)	20(3.60)	32(5.70)
Above 1500	30(5.40)	42(7.50)	28(5.00)	40(7.10)	58(10.40)
Total			**560(100)**		

Source : Computed from Primary Data

A text book or course book is a manual of instruction in schools. It is the most important teaching tool because it helps in attaining the school curriculum and facilitating the teaching learning process. Parents have to incur cost for text books and exercise books while making their children to get educate. Likewise stationery expenses should be incurred by the parents like pen, pencil, ruler, eraser, pencil box, note books, guides, charts etc. Almost six tenth of children get free text and exercise books from schools. So they incur only stationery expenses. 83 per cent of children were incurring less than Rs.500 per annum as books and stationery cost. At the same time RTE Act 2009 provides free text books and note books to students' up to elementary education and to some category students like SC / ST up to X classes. This helps the slum dwellers as well as low income households to have less financial burden in education.

A school uniform is a set of standardized clothes worn primarily for an educational institution. They form the basis of a school's dress code when used. Uniform costs for children attending private schools can be higher than other schools. The cost can vary dramatically as schools take a number of approaches to uniforms. More than one third of parents do not incur any cost on buying uniform materials. 20 per cent of children school outfit priced less than Rs.500. To slum dwellers uniforms were considered as a financial burden where it includes material costs as well as stitching costs. Provision of free uniform reduced these costs to some extent.

Getting a child to school safely and on time can be a challenge. Statutory walking distance is a threshold which determines the cost of home to school transport cost. Cost of transport incurred by slum parents depend on the mode of transportation. All children between 5 and 18 years entitled to free school transport however far they live from the school under RTE act. Around seven tenth children parents did not spent any cost for transportation. Nearly 13.40 per cent expenses between Rs.500-Rs.1000 and 10.40 per cent incurs more than Rs.1500 per annum as transport cost.

The aims of private tuition were to score more marks in the examination, to complete the homework, to do academic work and to cover untaught portion in the class. Slum parents are aware that their children were not provided good quality education as well as the teacher's motivation level is low and not taught properly in the school. To perform well in the school and also by looking at the mushrooming growth of tuition centres in the city, slum dwellers are also aware that their children cannot learn from the school alone. Parental education level is also lower, so they cannot help their children in doing routine school homework. So slum dwellers send their children to private tuitions which are becoming very popular now-a-days. More than one third of children were not taking private tuitions. Less than two third children were taking tuitions, 32.10 per cent parents spent less than Rs.500 per annum, 21.50 per cent expenses between Rs.500 to Rs.1000, 10.70 per cent incurred expenditure more than Rs.1000 on tuition per annum.

To find out the factors influencing child education chi square test has been applied with the help of demographic variables of urban slums. Religion of children did not emerge as an influencing factor for child education. The reason was that whatever be religion of children, the students for school enrolment are not taken into consideration.

Table 5.14 : Factor Influence on Child Education & Demographic Variables of Urban Slums

Demographic Variables	Chi square value	d.f	P value	Remark
Religion	7.603	2	0.422	Not Significant
Social groups	1.470	6	0.961	Not significant
Type of Family	3.366	2	0.186	Not Significant
Size of Family	4.093	4	0.004	Significant
Monthly family income (`)	11.706	4	0.011	Significant
Types of school	14.300	6	0.026	Significant
Distance of School	2.032	3	0.123	Not Significant
Annual expenditure of School	22.12	9	0.003	Significant
Living Environment Index(LEI)	15.12	8	0.002	Significant

Source : Computed from Primary Data

A social group is not as a factor influencing child education. School level education does not consider any distinction in case of community for enrolment. The relationship between child education and social groups was not significant.

Type of family, whether it was nuclear family or joint family, was not a significant factor in influencing child education. However, the nuclear family was having better chance to get better education in schools.

Size of family is also one of the factors influencing child education. It was expected that if family size increases, it needs to spend more on education by the family head. It was found that there was statistically significant difference between child education and size of family. If family size increases the head of the family was to allocate more resources for basic needs where allocation for education reduces and vice versa.

Monthly income of households is the major determinant of the child education. It is proved in the study that household's monthly income influences child education. When household income increases children are enrolled in better schools and given good education.

Types of school, annual school expenditure and living environment index are various factors influencing child education. Distance to school is not a factor influencing child education. Living environment index shows that with good environment child can concentrate on studies by regular attendance.

5.16 CONCLUSION

From the above analysis, it was helpful to understand the enrolment of children in different education standard as well as coverage was higher in entry level of schooling. Further it viewed about enrolment ratio; access to school; expenditure pattern and reasons for non-enrolment was mainly financial crisis. The existence of RTE resulted in reduction of schooling cost to convinced extent.

Chapter VI

HEALTH STATUS OF SLUM CHILDREN

6.1 INTRODUCTION

Health is a multi-dimensional and holistic, embracing aspects of individual and collective existence. It is considered as one of the basic rights of every human being irrespective of the race, religion, political beliefs, economic and social conditions. The health of slum dwellers is closely related to its social and economic status and political system. Good health of slum children would contribute towards improvement in educational attainment, higher income generation in their future in particular and overall economic development of the economy in general. So, the present chapter focuses on the health details of the respondents.

6.2 HEALTH STATUS OF THE RESPONDENTS

Health is a relative state in which one is able to function well physically, mentally, socially and spiritually in order to express the full range of one's unique potentialities within the environment in which one is living. Hence, an attempt has been made to study the health status of children.

Table 6.1 : Health Status of Children

Illness of Children	No. of Children	Per cent
Yes	350	56.45
No	270	43.55
Total	**620**	**100**

Source : Primary Data

The above table 6.1 explains that out of 620 samples, 56.45 per cent of children suffered from diseases and the remaining 43.55 percent of children have not suffered in the study area.

6.3 EFFECT OF ENVIRONMENT ON HEALTH

The environment has an effect on our health in a variety of ways. The relations between human health and the environmental risks have impact either directly by exposing people to harmful agents, or indirectly, by disrupting life-sustaining eco-systems. The major environmental jeopardy to health are connected with widespread poverty and severe lack of public infrastructure, such as access to drinking water, sanitation, and lack of health care as well as rising problems of pollution.

Based on this, it is necessary to analyse the type of disease the children suffered when we discuss the concept viz., health status. Hence the researcher is interested to study the nature of diseases the respondents suffered during the reference period (2014-2015) of survey. The following table 6.2 explores the type of health problems suffered by the children and living environment index in the above said reference period.

Table 6.2 : Type of Health Problem and Living Environment Index (LEI)

Standard of Living Index	**Low LEI**	**Medium LEI**	**High LEI**	**Total**
Type of Illness	**No. of Children (Per cent)**			
Cold, fever and head ache	70(44.00)	56(35.20)	33(20.80)	159(45.40)
Communicable Disease viz., malaria, diarrea, jaundice etc.	44(41.90)	32(30.50)	29(27.60)	105(30.00)
Skin problem	12(48.00)	8(32.00)	5(20.00)	25(7.10)
Anemia	5(50.00)	4(40.00)	1(10.00)	10(2.90)
Menstrual problems	9(50.00)	6(33.30)	3(16.70)	18(5.10)
Chronic problems	4(36.35)	4(36.35)	3(27.30)	11(3.20)
Others	10(45.45)	8(36.35)	4(18.20)	22(6.30)
Total	**154(44)**	**118(33.75)**	**78(22.25)**	**350(100)**
Chi-square	**20.66**			
Df	**13**			
P value	**.036***			

Source : Computed from Primary Data

Note : Figures in Parentheses are Percentages to the Row Total

*Denote at p value ≥ 0.05, significance at 10 percent

The type of illness children suffered were mostly comprised of common illness (45.40 per cent) such as cold, fever, head ache, while 30 per cent of children suffered due to communicable diseases like malaria, diarrhoea and jaundice. Among other diseases, skin problem were 7.10 per cent in the children, followed by menstrual problems (5.10 per cent), chronic diseases (3.20 per cent) such as asthma, malnutrition, developmental disabilities and anemia (2.90 per cent). 6.30 per cent suffered from other diseases like respiratory infections, mental illness, etc. Children living in low environment index (44 per cent) were the major sufferer of illness when compared to medium living environment index (33.75 per cent) and high living environment index (22.25 per cent). The National Sample Survey (NSS) 71st round reported that morbidity rate of slums is higher than the rate estimated for urban people in India. Children living in slums are 1.3 times more likely to suffer from diarrhea and fever than those in non-slum areas, which were reported as the two most common ailments in slums. This is reliable that the slum dwellers as a whole are relatively less healthy than the general population. Similar results were found in the study area that diarrhea and fever as the most common ailments suffered by children.

From the chi-square analysis on type of diseases and standard of living index that the 'p' value is less than 0.05 (0.036) the null hypothesis is rejected at 10 percent level of significance. Hence it is concluded that there is a significant association between the types of diseases of environmental factor like LEI.

6.4 APPROACH TO HOSPITAL

Hospital is an institution where health care provided to patient with specialized medical and nursing staff and medical equipment. The above table shows type of illness suffered by the respondents, in continuation of this, whether they approached hospital for health care treatment or not is depicted in table 6.3.

Table 6.3 : Approach to Hospital

Approach to Hospital	No. of Children	Percent
Yes	325	92.85
No	25	7.15
Total	**350**	**100**

Source : Primary Data

More than nine tenth of the respondents approached the hospitals for health care treatment whereas remaining 7.15 per cent of the respondent did not approached the hospital for health care treatment. The knowledge about the hospital's medical facilities made the slum households to visit the type of hospital.

6.5 TYPE OF HOSPITAL AND MONTHLY INCOME

Hospital plays a vital role in maintaining the well-being of the people. The World Health Organisation (WHO) defines modern hospitals as "A hospital is an integral part of social and medical organization, the function of which is to provide complete healthcare for the population, both curative and preventive and whose out-patient services reach out to the family and its home environment. The hospital is also a centre for training of health workers and for bio-social research". According to ownership, hospitals are divided into government hospitals and private hospitals. The government hospitals are owned, managed and controlled by the government whereas the private hospitals are owned by private parties. Government or public hospital may be medical college hospital, district hospital, city or town hospital and primary health centre. These hospitals provide treatment free of cost. Private hospital may be clinics, dispensary and specialized hospitals. These hospitals provide treatment for cost. Monthly income also determines the type of hospital the respondents approached for health care services. Thus it is depicted in the following table.

Table 6.4 : Type of Hospital and Monthly Income

Type of Hospital Monthly Income	Government	Private	PHC	Total
Less than Rs. 5000	67(39.20)	8(14.55)	40(40.40)	115(35.40)
Rs.5001-Rs.10000	45(26.30)	8(14.55)	26(26.30)	79(24.30)
Rs.10001-Rs.15000	32(18.70)	10(18.20)	14(14.20)	56(17.20)
Rs.15001-Rs.20000	17(10.00)	13(23.70)	10(10.10)	40(12.30)
Above Rs.20000	10(5.80)	16(29.00)	9(9.00)	35(10.80)
Total	**171(52.60)**	**55(16.90)**	**99(30.50)**	**325(100)**

Source : Computed from Primary Data

Note : Figures in Parentheses are Percentages to the Columns Total

More than 50 per cent of the respondents accessed government hospitals for their ailment. Around 30 per cent of the respondents utilized urban primary health centre for their treatment and remaining 16.90 per cent approached private hospitals for their illness. As the income of the respondents is low, they approached public hospitals due to free cost of treatment. Among the respondents approached government hospitals for treatment, 39.20 per cent of them were in monthly income of less than Rs.5000, followed by Rs.5001- Rs.10000 (26.30 per cent), Rs.10001- Rs.15000 (18.70 per cent), Rs.15001 – Rs.20000 (10 per cent) and above Rs.20000 (5.80 per cent). Of the total respondents who obtained treatment in private hospitals, 29 per cent of them were earning above Rs.20000 per month, followed by monthly income of Rs.15001 – Rs.20000 (23.70 per cent), Rs.5001- Rs.10000 (18.20 per cent), Rs.5001- Rs.10000 and less than Rs.5000 (14.55 per cent) each respectively.

The respondents who took treatment in primary health centre belongs to monthly income categories of less than Rs.5000 (35.40 per cent), followed by Rs.5001- Rs.10000 (24.30 per cent), Rs.10001- Rs.15000 (17.20 per cent), Rs.15001 – Rs.20000 (12.30 per cent) and above Rs.20000 (10.80 per cent). The respondents in higher income categories obtained treatment in private hospitals, because they are able to pay more for healthcare in these hospitals. A chi-square test was used and result of the test is also shown in the table 6.4a.

Table 6.4(a) : Type of Hospital and Monthly Family Income - Chi Square Test

Variables	Chi square Value	df	p	Remark
Type of hospital and Monthly Income	11.24	11	0.048	Significant**

Source : Primary Data

*Note : **denote at 10 percent*

It is noted from the above table 6.4a that the 'p' value is less than 0.05 and hence the result is significant at 10 per cent level. Hence the hypothesis rejected type of hospital and monthly family income. From the analysis it is concluded that there is significant association is found between the type of hospitals and monthly family income.

6.6 REASON FOR NOT APPROACH HOSPITAL

All the ill-health children are not taken to the hospital / clinics/ dispensaries for treatment. The reason may be inadequate money in hands during that time, simple disease and some may think it will cure by itself so not interested in giving treatment. So, the reason for not approach hospital is depicted in the following table.

Table 6.5 : Reason for not Approach Hospital

Reason	No. of Respondents	Percent
Economic Problems	8	32
Simple Diseases (Approach Medical)	12	48
Not Interested	5	20
Total	**25**	**100**

Source : Primary Data

Around 50 per cent of the respondents approached nearby medicals as they considered it as a simple disease. 32 per cent of the respondents did not approach the hospital due to economic problems and 20 per cent were not interested in taking treatment for illness. So no one reported that absence of health care services as reason for not accessing treatment.

6.7 KIND OF TREATMENT

There are different types of health care treatment systems like allopathy, ayurveda, homeopathy, naturopathy, etc. Allopathy is a kind of treatment, which aims to treat the illness and only focus on the symptoms not the causes. The patients have somehow been convinced that when sick, it is due to a lack of medicine or surgery and this is the only way. There is a pill for every ill, and even better, result in immediate relief from pain or illness. In India, homeopathy is an alternate and popular form of therapy. It is believed that like cures like means substances that cause diseases in healthy people, can cure them in sick people. In this system medication is delivered through solutions, which are poured onto homeopathic pills, which are then consumed. Siddha medicine is a form of traditional medicine which originated in Tamil Nadu. Disease is caused when the normal equilibrium of the three humors is disturbed. In this system of medicine, diet and lifestyle plays a major role in health and in curing diseases. Self / traditional medicine also refers to indigenous medicine. It consists of healing systems from a particular region or culture's traditional practices. It gives equal attention to body, mind and spirit.

It is significant to note that allopathic treatment is more common compared to homeopathy, siddha and self/traditional medicine. The details are provided in the following table 6.6.

Table 6.6 : Choice of Health Care Treatment

Choice of Health Care Treatment	No. of Respondents	Percent (%)
Allopathy	215	66.15
Homeopathy	22	6.75
Siddha	48	14.80
Self/Traditional Medicine	40	12.30
Total	**325**	**100**

Source : Primary Data

From this, about maximum three one (66.15 percent) of respondents preferred only allopathy treatment in urban slums. Nowadays, everybody prefers this treatment due to fast and immediate cure from the diseases. Similarly, minimum of respondents preferred siddha treatment (14.80 percent), Self/traditional medicine (12.30 percent) and homeopathy (6.75 percent) respectively.

6.8 NATURE OF TREATMENT

The nature of health problem and severity decides whether the children should be given inpatient or outpatient treatment. Inpatient means that the procedure requires the patient to be admitted to the hospital and stay overnight or for several days or weeks or months, primarily the patient can be closely monitored during the procedure and afterwards, during recovery. Some patients go to hospital for diagnosis, treatment or therapy, where the procedure does not require hospital admission and may also be performed outside the premises of a hospital is termed as outpatient. Thus the nature of treatment given is shown in the following table.

Table 6.7 : Nature of Treatment

Nature of Treatment	No. of Respondents	Percent (%)
Inpatient	72	22.15
Outpatient	253	77.85
Total	**325**	**100**

Source : Primary Data

Among 325 children, 77.85 per cent of them obtained outpatient health care treatment and remaining 22.15 per cent took inpatient health care treatment. More than half of the respondents suffered from common illness and various other diseases do not need inpatient care. Actually the patients do not have the option to pick between getting his care administered on an inpatient or an outpatient basis. The type of health care a patient receives completely based upon the health condition and physicians decision.

6.9 LENGTH OF STAY IN HOSPITAL

The length of stay in hospital describes the duration of hospitalization. Inpatients days are calculated from the day of admission to day of discharge in hospital. A shorter stay in hospital will reduce the cost of treatment and shift care from inpatients to less expensive post-acute settings. Thus the number of days stayed in hospital as inpatient is shown in the following table.

Table 6.8 : Length of Stay in Hospital

No. of Days	No. of Respondents	Percent (%)
Less than 2 Days	34	47.20
2-4 Days	16	22.30
4-7 Days	9	12.50
Above 7 Days	13	18.00
Total	**72**	**100**

Source : Primary Data

Nearly half of the respondents stayed for less than two days in hospital for treatment, followed by two to four days (22.30 percent), above 7 days (18 per cent) and four to seven days (12.50 per cent). The physicians believe that the patient must be kept under observation around the clock, or other specialized professional services or monitoring, or special equipment or facilities that only a hospital can provide. Thus type of diseases, severity, and recovery of patients decides the length of stay in hospital. The risk of medical complications like infections adds to the length of stay in hospital and also increases the cost of health care.

6.10 EXPENDITURES ON HEALTHCARE TREATMENT

The health spending can affect health conditions. It is important to note that the efficiency with which households are able to transform their spending into better health outcome varies significantly. To analyse the cost or expenditure on healthcare treatment by the sample respondents, the information has been collected with respect to various expenses during the treatment period. Further, total expenses have been categorised into three broad heads viz., pre-hospitalisation, hospitalisation and post-hospitalisation expenses. Each head includes both direct and indirect expenses under various components of expenses like doctor fees, lab fees, travel expenses, food, medicine and others. The following table 6.9 provides the different healthcare treatment expenditures.

Pre-hospitalisation expenditure refers to expenses incurred before hospitalization as well as outpatient treatment cost. During pre-hospitalisation, 28.90 per cent of the respondents had not incurred any expenses for treatment. 24.30 per cent of the respondents spent less than Rs.100, followed by Rs.251-500 (18.80 per cent), Rs.101-250 (17.50 per cent), Rs.501-1000 (8 per cent) and above Rs.1000 (2.50 per cent) for pre-hospitalisation expenses. The overall average expenditures of the respondents during pre-hospitalisation were Rs.240.15.

Table 6.9 : Expenditures on Healthcare Treatment

Expenses (Rs.)	Categories of Expenses		
	Pre-Hospitalization Expenses	Hospitalization Expenses	Post-Hospitalization Expenses
NIL	94(28.90)	253(77.90)	260(80.00)
Less than 100	79(24.30)	4(1.20)	27(8.30)
101-250	57(17.50)	9(2.80)	16(4.90)
251-500	61(18.80)	12(3.70)	11(3.40)

Expenses (Rs.)	Categories of Expenses		
	Pre-Hospitalization Expenses	**Hospitalization Expenses**	**Post-Hospitalization Expenses**
501-1000	26(8.00)	18(5.50)	7(2.20)
Above1000	8(2.50)	29(8.90)	4(1.20)
Average	**240.15**	**568.40**	**180.60**
Total		**325(100)**	

Source : Computed from Primary Data

Note : Figures in Parentheses are Percentages to the Column Total

Hospitalization expenditure is the cost incurred by inpatient for treatment. Some of the respondents were hospitalised, so it is necessary to study hospitalization expenditure of healthcare treatment. More than 75 per cent of the respondents had not incurred any hospitalization expenses. The remaining less than one fourth of the respondents spent less than Rs.100 (1.20 per cent), Rs.101-250 (2.80 per cent), Rs.251-500 (3.70 per cent), Rs.501-1000 (5.50 per cent) and above Rs.1000 (8.90 per cent). The average expenditure on hospitalization of healthcare treatment was Rs.568.40 in the study area.

The third category of expenditure on healthcare treatment is post-hospitalisation expenditure. It refers to expenditure incurred by inpatients after hospitalization for treatment. Nearly fourth fifth (80 per cent) of the respondents had not incurred any expenses in post-hospitalisation healthcare treatment. Next to this, 8.30 per cent of the respondents spent less than Rs.100 only. Only 4.90 and 3.40 per cent respondents incurred expenses of Rs.101-250 and Rs.251-500 respectively. About 3.40 per cent respondents spent above Rs.500 as post-hospitalisation expenditure. The average post-hospitalisation expenditure of the respondents was calculated as Rs.180.60.

6.11 LOSS OF INCOME OF CAREGIVERS OR PARENTS

Cost of healthcare treatment measures all the costs of a particular disease includes both the direct and indirect costs. The previous table explains the direct cost incurred by the respondents during illness. In continuation of that, the indirect costs are measured in terms of foregone earnings or opportunity cost. The respondents are in dependent age group; it is necessary to calculate the foregone earnings of caregivers or parents during illness of children. Hence the foregone earnings are measured in terms of wages lost by parents per day. During pre-hospitalisation, hospitalisation and post-hospitalisation, the information about the foregone income of both for demanders and non-demanders of healthcare treatment is given in the following table.

Table 6.10 : Foregone Earnings of Parents (per day)

Income (Rs.)	No. of Respondents	Percent (%)
Nil	179	55.10
Up to 100	38	11.70
101 to 250	54	16.60
251-500	35	10.80
Above 500	19	5.80
Total	**325**	**100**

Source : Primary Data

The above table 6.10 explains that more than half (55.10 per cent) of the respondent's parents were not foregone any earnings or zero opportunity cost because the parents were going to hospital only in the evening time or non-working mother took them to hospital. Less than one fifth (16.60 per cent) of parents foregone earnings was Rs.101 to 250 per day. Next to this, more than one tenth (11.70 per cent) of the respondent's parents opportunity cost was up to Rs.100 per day, followed by Rs.251 to 500 (10.80 per cent) and above Rs.500 (5.80 per cent). The higher opportunity cost reflects higher labour force participation rates and earnings by male parents. The parents foregone work days differ from respondents to respondents based upon the healthcare treatment.

6.12 DISTANCE TO HOSPITAL

Various researches revealed that the average distance between patients' homes and the hospitals in which they receive healthcare have barely changed for a decade. The distance to hospital, journey time and patient condition also decides the healthcare treatment of children. It is shown in the following table.

Table 6.11 : Distance to Hospital

Distance(Km.)	No. of Respondents	Percent
Less than 1	166	51.00
2-3	88	27.10
Above 3	71	21.90
Total	**325**	**100**

Source : Computed from Primary Data

More than half of the respondents travel less than 1 kilometer to hospital for treatment purpose. In the remaining one half of respondents, 27.10 per cent move nearly 2 to 3 kilometers and 21.90 per cent pass through above 3 kilometers to reach the hospital. Healthcare expenditure includes direct costs like travel cost also, if travel distance increases the cost incurred by the patient also increases. Thus no one reported that hospital is far away to reach or not within the reachable limit. This shows the availability of healthcare facilities within the reach of people; either it can be public or private health care system.

Table 6.12 : Distribution of Slum Households by Distance from Nearest Health Centre Compare with NSS Data

Distance (in km)	NSS Rounds				Primary Data
	49th Round	**58th Round**	**65th Round**	**69th Round**	
Less than 0.5	29.8	21.1	20.2	20.3	22.3
0.5 – 1	33.2	26.2	27.9	27.3	27.7
1 - 2	15.2	23.2	22.9	17.1	18.1
2 – 5	17.7	24.9	20.8	23.8	20.0
5 and above	4.1	4.6	8.2	11.5	11.9
Total	100	100	100	100	100

Source : Primary Data

National Sample Survey Office (NSSO), NSS Report No: 417, 486, 534 & 561

The nearness of health centre to slum household trend is shown in table. The distance from nearest health centre to slum households was very low in 2009 as compared to 1993. In 49th round NSSO survey 63 per cent slum households had health centers within 1 km distance. But, the same decreased to 47 per cent in 2002, 48 per cent in 2009 and 2012. In 1993, the nearest health centre was available within 1 to 5 km distance for 32 per cent of slum households; this was 48 per cent in 2002, 43 per cent in 2009 and 41 per cent in 2012. When primary data compared with NSSO survey rounds shows more or less the same distance from nearest health centre.

6.13 PERFORMANCE OF HEALTH CARE SERVICES

The last objective of this study is that to find out the health status of slums children. With regards health care services one of the important factors determinants of health status. Along with this the available infrastructure facilities also captured such as, operation theater, lab facilities, bed, fan, pharmacist, water and toilet facilities, attenders rest room, space for outpatient, space for inpatient, ambulance services and canteen facilities. The variables which we have taken for the performance analysis are qualitative in nature. Hence, 4 point scaling technique has been adopted viz, Poor, Moderate, Good and Not accessible, for each and every services with respect to hospital services. The following table gives the detail of the variables and the weightage assigned to each variable.

Table 6.13 : Details of Health Care Service

Health Care Service	Weight Ages Assigned to Each Variables				Total
	Poor -1	**Moderate-2**	**Good- 3**	**Not -** Accessible-0	
Performance of Doctor	10(3.00)	35(10.80)	**280(86.20)**	-	325 (100)
Performance of Nurse	15(4.60)	22(6.80)	**288(88.60)**	-	325 (100)
Performance of Lab Technician	40(12.40)	49(15.00)	**236(72.60)**	-	325 (100)
Medicine service	17(5.20)	28(8.60)	**280(86.20)**	-	325 (100)
Fees Structure	20(6.20)	28(8.60)	**277(85.20)**	-	325 (100)

Health Care Service	**Weight Ages Assigned to Each Variables**				Total
	Poor -1	**Moderate-2**	**Good- 3**	**Not - Accessible-0**	
Operation theatre services	75(23.00)	90(27.70)	**130(40.00)**	30(9.30)	325 (100)
Lab Facilities	**105(32.40)**	80(24.60)	75(23.00)	65(20.00)	325 (100)
Drinking Water Facilities	123(37.90)	**142(43.70)**	60(18.40)	-	325 (100)
Toilet Facilities	**165(50.80)**	100(30.80)	60(18.40)	-	325 (100)
Space for outpatient	55(17.00)	108(33.20)	**162(49.80)**	-	325 (100)
Space for inpatient	110(33.90)	**130(40.00)**	85(26.10)	-	325 (100)
Bed Facilities	62(19.00)	**138(42.50)**	125(38.50)	-	325 (100)
Fan Facilities	25(7.70)	45(13.90)	**240(73.80)**	15(4.60)	325 (100)
Attenders rest room	**153(47.00)**	40(12.30)	48(14.80)	84(25.90)	325 (100)
Ambulance Services	10(3.00)	25(7.70)	**270(83.10)**	20(6.20)	325 (100)
Canteen Facilities	60(18.50)	25(7.70)	20(6.10)	**220(67.70)**	325 (100)
Overall Opinion about this services	66(20.30)	79(24.30)	**180(55.40)**	-	325 (100)

Source : Computed from Primary Data

Figures in the Parentheses are Percentage to the Row Total

The above table, it shows that most of the respondents say that doctor performance (86.20 percent), performance of nurse (88.60 percent), performance of lab technician (72.60 percent), medicine (86.20 per cent), fees structure (85.20 percent), operation theatre services (40.00 percent), space for outpatient (49.80 percent), fan facilities (73.80 percent), ambulance services (83.10 percent), overall opinion (55.40 percent) are good. In this connection, majority of the respondents say that drinking water facilities (43.70 percent), space for inpatient (49.80 percent), bed facilities (42.50 percent) are moderate. Next of this, poor opinion of health care service were found in lab facilities (32.40 per cent), toilet facilities (50.80 per cent) and attendee's rest room (47 per cent). About 67.70 per cent reported that canteen facilities are not accessible in nature.

6.14 FACTORS INFLUENCE OF HEALTH STATUS OF URBAN SLUMS CHILDREN

Further, an attempt was made to find out the determinants of health status among the children. The endogenous factor used to run the regression analysis was child health status which was derived by framed equation. The exogenous variables were selected with the help of theoretical support and the previous works. The child health status function was erected as following.

$$CHS = \beta_0 + \beta_1 X_{1i} + \beta_2 X_{2i} + \ldots\ldots\ldots\ldots\ldots + \beta_k X_{ki} + Ui$$

where,

SE = Children Health Status

B_0 = Constant,

X_{1i} to X_{ki} explains the explanatory variables used in the study,

β_1 to β_k explains the co-efficient value of respective exogenous variables.

Ui = error term

After running the ordinary least square (OLS) regression to make the results reliable, various OLS assumptions were checked by applying Correlation Matrix (to check multi-collinearity problem exists), normality test, (to prove the normal distribution of variables), heteroscedasticity (to prove the variance of each $U_i = 0$), etc. By doing these tests, it was proved that maximum of the OLS assumptions were fulfilled. Hence, it could be said that the result driven from the OLS regression is reliable and unbiased. The following table 6.13 gives brief information about the variables which are determining the child socioeconomic and living environment index variables and the expected sign also.

Table 6.14 : Variables Included and their Expected Sign

Code of the Variable	Variable Type	Expansion of the Code	Expected Sign
AG	Q	Age of the Children(Years)	+
CEDU	D	Child Education Level	
CEDU-1		Primary =1; Otherwise=0	
CEDU-2		Middle =1; Otherwise =0	
CEDU-3		Secondary =1; Otherwise =0	-
CEDU-4		Higher Secondary =1; Otherwise=0	
NSC	Q	Number of School Going Children	-
SX	D	Sex of the Children	
		Male =1; Female=1	+
RG		Religion of the Children	+
RG-1	D	Hindu=1; Otherwise =0	
RG-2		Christian =1; Otherwise =0	
RG-3		Muslim =1; Otherwise =0	
CM		Community of the Children	
CM-1		Backward Community =1 Otherwise =0	
CM-2	D	Most Backward Community =1 Otherwise =0	+
CM-3		Schedule Caste/Schedule Tribe =1 Otherwise =0	
TF	D	Type of Family	+
		Joint Family =1; Otherwise=0	
SF	Q	Size of the Family (Number)	+
HMI	Q	Household Monthly Income(Rs.)	+
HME	Q	Household Monthly Expenditure(Rs.)	+

Code of the Variable	Variable Type	Expansion of the Code	Expected Sign
FOCC		Father Occupation	
FOCC-1	D	Daily Worker	
FOCC-2		Private Worker	
FOCC-3		Self Employed	
FOCC-4		Govt. Job	+
FOCC-5		Others	
P-EDU		Parental Education	
PEDU-1	D	Illiterate =1; Otherwise=0	
PEDU-2		Primary =1; Otherwise=0	
PEDU-3		Secondary =1; Otherwise =0	
PEDU-4		Degree and Above =1; Otherwise =0	+
TS	D	Type of School	
TS-1		Government School =1; Otherwise =0	
TS-2		Aided School =1; Otherwise =0	
TS-3		Private School =1; Otherwise =0	-
LEI		Living Environment Index(LEI)	
LEI-1	D	Low LEI=1; Otherwise=0	-
LEI-2		Medium LEI=1, Otherwise=0	
LEI-3		High LEI=1, Otherwise=0	

Note : D - Dummy variable and Q - Quantitative Variable

The above table 6.13 explains the different variables related to health status of slum children. With a view to analyse the factor, which determines the health status, the researcher collected the child related variables and presented the descriptive statistics of the above said independent variables. To study the determinants of health status of slum children, the researcher used Ordinary Least Square (OLS) method by using the illness of health in children as dependent variables. Before discussing regression analysis, we shall look into the mean and standard deviation of the independent variables. The following table 6.14 explains the exogenous and endogenous variables.

Table 6.15 : Descriptive Statistics of Independent Variables

Variables	Minimum	Maximum	Mean	Standard deviation
Age of the Children(Years)	5	18	13.151	5.1011
Child Education Level	1	12	9.103	2.1024
Number of School Going Children	1	4	1.17	1.051
Sex of the Children	.00	1.00	.5793	.49418
Religion of the Children	1	3	1.35	.688
Community of the Children	1	4	3.08	.792
Type of Family	1	2	1.70	.459
Size of the Family (Number)	1	9	4.29	1.445
Household Monthly Income(Rs.)	2000	32200	11424.12	5756.556
Household Monthly Expenditure(Rs.)	1800	6132	2155.414	737.234
Type of School	1	3	1.30	1.519
Living Environment Index(LEI)				
Low	.00	1.00	.4130	.42491
Medium	.00	1.00	.3252	.45404
High	.00	1.00	.1218	.31892

6.15 FACTORS DETERMINING THE HEALTH STATUS OF SLUMS CHILDREN

It is explained from the regression analysis table 6.15 that the relationship between the dependent and independent variables was statistically significant. It could be interpreted from the R^2 value and it is given in this table that the endogenous variables were explained by the exogenous variables in the 0.514 respectively.

Table 6.16 : Factors Determining the Health Status of Slums Children

Code of the Variable	Variable Type	Expansion of the code	Co efficient	't' value
Constant				8.655
AG	Q	Age of the Children(Years)	0.066	2.690**
Child Education Level				
CEDU-1		Primary =1; Otherwise=0	0.053	-2.135***
CEDU-2		Middle =1; Otherwise =0	0.255	1.122
CEDU-3		Secondary =1; Otherwise =0	0.325	1.562
CEDU-4	D	Higher Secondary =1; Otherwise=0	0.128	2.018***
NSC	Q	Number of School Going Children	0.236	-0.298***
SX	D	Sex of the Children Male =1; Female=1	0.074	0.865
Religion of the Children				
RG-1		Hindu=1; Otherwise =0	0.003	3.004*
RG-2	D	Christian =1; Otherwise =0	0.762	0.519
RG-3		Muslim =1; Otherwise =0	0.475	0.278
Community of the Children				

Code of the Variable	Variable Type	Expansion of the code	Co efficient	't' value
CM-1	D	Backward Community =1 Otherwise =0	0.033	4.009*
CM-2		Most Backward Community =1 Otherwise =0	0.235	0.237***
CM-3		Schedule Caste/Schedule Tribe =1 Otherwise =0	-0.034	3.316*
TF	D	Type of Family		
		Joint Family =1; Otherwise=0	0.135	1.127
SF	Q	Size of the Family (Number)	0.025	-0.316*
HMI	Q	Household Monthly Income(Rs.)	2.607	4.812*
HME	Q	Household Monthly Expenditure(Rs.)	2.230	2.208**
Father Occupation				
FOCC-1		Daily Worker	0.343	-2.242**
FOCC-2		Private Worker	0.022	0.394
FOCC-3		Self Employed	-0.113	0.534
FOCC-4		Government Employed	0.307	2.418**
FOCC-5	D	Others	0.522	1.025
Parental Education				
PEDU-1		Illiterate =1; Otherwise=0	0.212	-1.314***
PEDU-2	D	Primary =1; Otherwise=0	0.325	0.758
PEDU-3		Secondary =1; Otherwise =0	0.623	1.034

Code of the Variable	Variable Type	Expansion of the code	Co efficient	't' value
PEDU-4		Degree and Above =1; Otherwise =0	0.107	3.528*
Type of School				
TS-1		Government School =1; Otherwise =0	0.0245	1.028
TS-2		Aided School =1; Otherwise =0	0.854	1.175
TS-3	D	Private School =1; Otherwise =0	0.214	2.654***
Living Environment Index(LEI)				
LEI-1		Low LEI=1; Otherwise=0	0.041	0.624
LEI-2	D	Medium LEI=1, Otherwise=0	0.463	1.275**
LEI-3		High LEI=1, Otherwise=0	0.362	3.397*

Source : Computed from Primary Data

Note: * *Significant at 1 per cent level*
** *Significant at 5 per cent level*
*** *Significant at 10 per cent level*

Table 6.15 presents the estimated coefficients and 'p' values for school going children in urban slums. As expected, the age of the children was significantly associated with the health status of in study area. High aged children were much more health status than the low aged school going children. This may be due to fact that increasing age of children had positive significant effect on health status of urban slums.

The regression indicated the participation of **children in school programs**. The researcher classified into four, such as primary, middle, secondary and higher secondary. Primary school going children have been negatively significantly influence at 10 percent. Therefore, higher secondary school going children have been positively significant at 10 percent. In this connection middle and secondary school going children did not influence on health status of urban slums. However, it was found from the result higher educated school going children better health status compare than low educated school going children.

The other categories of independent variable such as **number of school going children** in household has negatively influence at 10 percent level. It is observed that it may be due to the reason of dependency ration and also intra-household and other health facility among the family members include children. The gap between one children and another children is also very less between the children.

In this connection middle and secondary school going children did not influence on health status of urban slums.

The sex of the children did not influence on health status of urban slums. On other hand the religion of children in urban slums. The Hindu religion of children has significant at 1 percent and positive effect on health status. And another religion such as, Christian and Muslim did not influence on health status in urban slums.

The dummy variable representing a **social status of children** in the study area, the backward community and most backward community had positive significant at 1 percent and 10 percent. On other hand, schedule caste and schedule tribes had negative effect on health status at 1 percent. In reason behind that, most of these schedule caste and schedule tribes households parents are working as daily wage earners; hence it is evident that the these community people are living very low level economic condition of urban slums.

The types of family not have influence on child health status. On other hand size of family has negatively influence at 1 percent level. It is observed that it may be due to the reason of increase dependency ratio, the distribution of intra-households food, nutritional and basic facilities are very low in urban households.

The family **monthly income and expenditure** are correlated variables of the basic economy of households. As the level of income increases there is an increase in increase on household's expenditure. The above regression analysis shows that monthly income of households has a positive effect on weight-for-age at 1 percent level. In general high income earning households can spend more amount on the special nutrient food items compared to low earning households in the study area.

It was expected that **expenditure on family** would positively influence at 5 percent level. Therefore, expenditure per month include food expenditure incurred by the households was added as an important variable affecting the child health status. The researcher observed and investigated that most of the household's total expenditure allocation was high in the food expenses following the other expenses.

Another socio-economic variable of **father's occupation** is one of the important factors determined by the child health status. A daily worker has negatively significant influence at 5 percent. Occupation of government employment of father has positive effect on health status at 5 percent. On other hand private, self and other occupation father did not influence on health status of children. Basically daily wage worker father have low level earning and low time to spent on child care activities. Hence, government working men are having better nutrition knowledge, health education and income earning in the study area

Parental education appears to improve the child's health status. The above table summarizes the results and shows that above illiterate **education of father and mother** has negatively effect on health status at 10 percent. Nevertheless education degree and above had a positive significant effect on 1 percent. Next of this, parental education on primary and secondary education does not have a significant effect on health status. The researcher observed that well educated parents have a significant effect on health status in the study area because both mother and father are monitoring the child's activity and consumption of nutrient food.

As expected, the **type of school** going the children in slums area. The researcher categorized their participation into two, such as government, aided and private school. The private school going children have been positively significantly influenced at 10 percent on health status. However, it was found from the result private school going children have a better health influence than other school going children.

Among the household living environment variables medium standard of living index has a positive significance at 5 percent on health status. Next to this, high standard of living index has a positive significant influence at each 1 percent level on urban children health status. Children from those households which use good urban slums household facilities such as toilet, drinking water, sanitation facilities have positive impact on health status. The poor slums household's facility should be affected by children on various health problems like malaria, diarrea, skin and other problem.

From the regression analysis, it is summarized that the explanatory variables which positively influenced health status of children are age of children, child education, number of school going children, religion, social status, family income, family expenditure, father occupation, parental education type of school and standard of living index. Similarly variables which influence negatively are child education, social status, family size, father occupation and parental education.

The hypothesis test of the above analysis shows the factor determining the health status of urban slums children. The result is that the 'p' value is less than 0.05 and the null hypothesis is accepted at 1 percent, 5 percent and 10 percent level of various factors such as (children are age of children, child education, number of school going children, religion, social status, family income, family expenditure, father occupation, parental education and type of school) of the study area. On the other hand 'p' value is greater than 0.05 and the result is not significant at 1 percent 5 and 10 percent level of child education, social status, family size, father occupation and parental education. Hence, it is concluded that there is a strong significant influence of various above said factors on the health status of urban slum children.

Another important hypothesis is that there is a positive association between households living environment condition and health status of slums children. Since 'p' value is less than 0.05, the null hypothesis is accepted at 5 and 1 percent level of significance. Hence, it is concluded that there is strong significant influence on the health status and slums households living environment condition.

6.16 CONCLUSION

This chapter finally concludes with the analysis and results of the health variables such as type of illness, type and kind of treatment, reasons for not approach to hospital, length of stay in hospital, expenditures on healthcare treatment, loss of income of caregivers or parents, distance to hospital, performance of health care services, factors determining the health status of slum children. In this connection the following chapter deals with the summary of findings, suggestions and conclusion of the present study.

Chapter VII

SUMMERY OF FINDINGS AND CONCLUSION

7.1 INTRODUCTION

An unprecedented pace and scale of urbanization is witnessed by India, which results in the insufficient delivery of urban infrastructure and basic services to have citizens a decent quality of life. Urban India suffers from inadequate housing stock and is highly congested and polluted by underserved utilities. Increasing urban population put enormous stress on the urban system by mushrooming of slums. Slums represent informal settlements in urban areas, yet provide shelter to a large proportion of economically productive work force, which contributes in significant measure to the economic growth of the nation. Thus the existence of slums is really associated with development process especially rapid urbanization.

As underserved utilities in such areas, this neglected population has become a major reservoir for a wide spectrum of health conditions. Because of informal native of slum settlements, cultural, social and behavioural factors, and these people is little known about the spectrum, burden and determinants of illnesses which give rise to spread of chronic, communicable and infectious diseases results in complications among the slum children.

In India, every child up to the age of 14 is entitled to free schooling, but in slums as children grow up, lack of encouragement from parents as well as economic pressure to leave school made them to start working. Thus the majority of children leave school by the age of 16. The most common belief among slum residents about higher education that even completing school is that it's a waste of time and money.

With these concerns, the problem of the study was formulated and it was intended to analyse the following objectives.

- To study the socio-economic status (SES) and living environment conditions of the respondents in urban slums.
- To analyses education attainment of children in schools in urban slums.
- To find out the health status of children and performance of health care system in the study area.

In this chapter, the findings of the data analysis have been summerised and conclusion is given. The findings are presented hereby - objective wise.

SOCIO-ECONOMIC BACKGROUND OF THE SAMPLE CHILDREN

More than two-third (71.90 per cent) of the slum dwellers were in productive age group above 15 years. Nearly 28 per cent were in unproductive age group less than 15 years. Around 29 per cent and 23 per cent fall under age categories of 16-30 years and 31-45 years.

A glimpse at the sex ratio shows that male outnumbered female only by one per cent. 50.50 per cent were male population and residual were female (49.50 per cent).

It was found that more than two-fifth (42 per cent) slum dwellers were unmarried and left over were married (58 per cent). Among married around 2 per cent were divorced / widow / separated.

Though less than one third (28.3 per cent) slum dwellers was illiterate, more than 14 per cent had higher secondary and above. Around 20 per cent had primary education and 34.67 per cent of them had middle and secondary level education.

Majority of slum dwellers were non-workers (56.54 per cent) which include students, housewife and others. It exhibits that more than 20 per cent were students. It can be observed that more than 40 per cent of the slum dwellers were engaged in various types of activities, mostly of unskilled works.

Around 26 per cent of the slum dwellers were daily wage workers, while one of every 8 slum dwellers were engaged in construction works. Less than 10 per cent of slum dwellers were salaried workers and nearly 8 per cent of them were self employed.

It was known that more than half (56.54 per cent) of the household members were non-earning dependents and the rest were earning members. Among the total individual members, nearly one fifth of them were earning less than Rs.5000 per month, around 5 per cent were in above Rs.10001 income group and the left over 16 per cent of members were earning monthly income Rs.5001- Rs.10000.

Around 75 per cent of the slum dwellers belonged to Hindu and the rest of the respondents belonged to Christian (10.20 per cent) and Muslims (12.20 per cent).

Among the total sample households, around 35 per cent of the households hailed from Most Backward Class as well as Scheduled Caste/ Scheduled Tribes.

Only 30 per cent of slum dwellers were attached with joint family system and the remaining were living as nuclear family.

The most dominant family size among the respondents were 4-5 members which alone constitute 52 per cent to the total, followed by the family size of less than 3 members (29.20 per cent). The number of respondents, who had the family size above 5 members constituted 18.80 per cent. The mean size of the family members was found 4 only.

Out of the total, 34.50 per cent of the households earned monthly income between Rs.10001-Rs.15000, while 32.80 per cent of the households were making income in the range of Rs.5001- Rs.10000 per month.

Nearly 9 per cent of them save monthly between Rs.101 – Rs.500, while 4.80 per cent of the respondents were saving in the range of 0- Rs.100 and 4.2 per cent save more than Rs.501 per month.

It was revealed that a more than 55 per cent of the slum dwellers reside in porumbok land or public land for many years. Only few inhabitants claimed ownership of land from the government and got patta.

With respect to property value of slum households depicted that majority did not possess any assets (77.80 per cent), about 12 per cent of respondents were holding property value more than Rs.150000.

Most of slum dwellers were non migrants (85 per cent) and the left behind were migrants. Among migrants, 10 per cent of the respondents were migrants from different districts inside Tamil Nadu and the rest (5 per cent) were from other states.

Of the total migrants, nearly 4 per cent migrants reported better employment opportunity as reason for it. It was followed by poverty (8 per cent), better education for their children (3 per cent) and only a few respondents stated as crazy for urban living (1 per cent).

The slum dwellers were inhabited in these areas for long periods of time. Majority of respondents (37.20 per cent) were inhabited for 21 to 30 years.

LIVING ENVIRONMENT OF THE SLUM DWELLERS

Among the respondents, nearly 55 per cent had pucca houses, followed by semi pucca houses (31 per cent) and only 14 per cent of the slum households had katcha houses.

More than 40 per cent families live in one room houses and that single room is used as bed room, sitting room, dining room, kitchen and store as living room or common room.

Nearly three fifth of the respondents does not have separate kitchen while the remaining two fifth have separate room for cooking.

Almost two third of the respondents were fetching water through street tap. The remaining one third of them were getting water from tank water (19.50 per cent), own tap (8.20 per cent) and other sources (5.80 per cent).

Nearly about all of the respondents (92 per cent) stated that they have electricity in their houses.

It was revealed that a 72.50 per cent of the respondent rooms have just one window mostly of small size and the rest (27.50 per cent) have no window in their small room.

It was found that the 83.25 per cent of them use mosquito repellents and 16.75 per cent did not use anything to defense it.

More than 50 per cent of the respondents use LPG for cooking, 17 per cent make use of kerosene and stove for cooking, 12.20 per cent employ wood as fuel in hand made oven, 10.50 per cent use fire wood and LPG in this purpose, 6.5 per cent utilize both fire wood and kerosene.

Almost all the respondents possess any one of the durable goods listed above. 11.50 per cent have radio, 90 per cent possess television, 87.50 per cent own electric fan, 75.75 per cent hold mobile phone, 22.50 per cent acquire refrigerator, 64.75 per cent obtain bicycle, 66.75 per cent possess grinder/mixer, 51.25 per cent have motorcycle and 18.25 per cent of the households own other assets such as washing machine, cupboard, chair, coolers, cot, sewing machine, etc.

More than half of the drainage system existed in the slum households were open katcha (56.20 per cent) followed by open pucca (19 per cent) constructed of pucca materials such as cement, bricks, etc.

Almost 46.50 per cent of households use public toilet and around one fourth of slum households have their own toilet facility. Nearly one fifth of them use open space for defecation purpose and only 5 per cent sharing toilets with their neighbourhoods.

With respect to about 86 per cent of slum households did not have bath room and nearly one seventh avail this facility.

About 70 per cent of slum households have access to municipal corporation dustbin for garbage disposal. Nearly 22 per cent of them do not have any arrangement so dumped garbage in unused open place nearby their houses such as roadside, ditches, drain, etc.

Space for cleaning and drying clothes in slum houses were totally absent in 58 per cent of the households and they use little space in front of houses or streets for this purpose.

In most slums, roads are motorable approach. About 55.30 per cent of slums had semi pucca road, followed by pucca (26.50 per cent) and katcha or absence of road (18.20 per cent) inside the slums.

More than 90 per cent of the slum households reported availability of stand lamps in their street and in the remaining cases absence of light sources in the streets

Most of the households were in low LEI (45 per cent) followed by medium LEI (37 per cent) and the remaining were in high LEI. Low LEI indicated that these slum dwellers were deprived of access to basic services such as water, fuel, sanitation, etc.

EDUCATION OF SLUM CHILDREN

It was found that among male children, 93.35 per cent were enrolled in schools and remaining 6.65 per cent were dropout from schools. Out of total female children, 85.65 per cent were enrolled in different school levels and remaining 14.35 per cent were dropped out.

Among enrolled children, 33.50 per cent were enrolled in higher secondary level, followed by secondary level (23.90 per cent), primary level (23.40 per cent) and middle level (19.20 per cent)

Dropout was higher in secondary school level both in case of male (56 per cent) and female children (51.40 per cent).

Most of the slum children enrolled in government school alone made up 65.20 per cent followed by aided school (30 per cent) and remaining in private schools (4.80 per cent).

Nearly one tenth (9.70 per cent) were dropped out from schools. Dropout was higher in government schools (56.70 per cent) and followed by aided schools (43.30 per cent).

Almost 40.60 per cent of children in income group less than Rs.5000 were attending government schools. Private schools (30 per cent) were more catering for the need of income categories Rs.10001- Rs.15000.

About one fifth children were sent to school to get better employment opportunities in the future; nearly 14.30 per cent children parents stated provision of free mid-day meals schemes was also an indirect reason for school enrolment.

With respect to 92 per cent of them were regularly attending the schools and 8 per cent of children were not attending the schools regularly.

Nearly 26.60 per cent of children were absent due to their sickness, more than one tenth were not interested in attending school due to insufficient coaching, less than one tenth stated lack of parents motivation to attend school regularly, one fifth of the absentees were poor performer in class and 17.80 per cent reported that children had gone to their native place.

More than two fifth of the children were forced to leave school due to family crisis i.e. financial crisis or poverty, less than one fifth were out of school due to lack of interest in their studies, almost one third dropped out as they started work to support their family. Around 3.33 per cent of children never attended the school due to acute health syndrome.

The average earnings of the employed children were Rs. 3278 per month.

With respect to distance to reach school, three fifth of children have to journey between 1-3 kms distance whereas one fourth of kids have to travel within 1 km from their habitat or residence.

It was found that 32.10 per cent of children were deemed to be within walkable distance to school, so to cover the distance either they walked or used bicycles.

More than one fourth of parents remitted less than Rs.500 as tuition fee. 83 per cent of children were incurring less than Rs.500 per annum as books and stationery cost.

Around seven tenth children parents did not spent any cost for transportation. More than one third of children were not taking private tuitions.

Types of school, annual school expenditure and living environment index are various factors influencing child education. Religion of children, social groups, type of family and distance of school did not emerge as an influencing factor for child education.

HEALTH STATUS OF SLUM CHILDREN

It was known that 56.45 per cent of children suffered from diseases and the remaining 43.55 percent of children have not suffered in the study area.

The type of illness children suffered were mostly comprised of common illness (45.40 per cent) such as cold, fever, head ache, while 30 per cent of children suffered due to communicable diseases like malaria, diarrhoea and jaundice.

Children living in low environment index (44 per cent) were the major sufferer of illness when compared to medium living environment index (33.75 per cent) and high living environment index (22.25 per cent).

More than nine tenth of the respondents approached the hospitals for health care treatment whereas remaining 7.15 per cent of the respondent did not approached the hospital for health care treatment.

It was known that 50 per cent of the respondents accessed government hospitals for their ailment. Around 30 per cent of the respondents utilized urban primary health centre for their treatment.

Approached government hospitals for treatment, 39.20 per cent of them were in monthly income of less than Rs.5000.

Around 50 per cent of the respondents approached nearby medicals as they considered it as a simple disease.

From this, about maximum three one (66.15 percent) of respondents preferred only allopathy treatment in urban slums.

Among 325 children, 77.85 per cent of them obtained outpatient health care treatment and remaining 22.15 per cent took inpatient health care treatment.

Nearly half of the respondents stayed for less than two days in hospital for treatment, followed by two to four days (22.30 percent), above 7 days (18 per cent) and four to seven days (12.50 per cent).

It was found that about 28.90 per cent of the respondents had not incurred any expenses for treatment. 24.30 per cent of the respondents spent less than Rs.100. The overall average expenditures of the respondents during pre-hospitalisation were Rs.240.15.

More than 75 per cent of the respondents had not incurred any hospitalization expenses. The remaining less than one fourth of the respondents spent less than Rs.100 (1.20 per cent). The average expenditure on hospitalization of healthcare treatment was Rs.568.40 in the study area.

Nearly fourth fifth (80 per cent) of the respondents had not incurred any expenses in post-hospitalisation healthcare treatment. Next to this, 8.30 per cent of the respondents spent less than Rs.100 only. The average post-hospitalisation expenditure of the respondents was calculated as Rs.180.60.

More than half (55.10 per cent) of the respondent's parents were not foregone any earnings or zero opportunity cost because the parents were going to hospital only in the evening time or non-working mother took them to hospital.

More than half of the respondents travel less than 1 kilometer to hospital for treatment purpose. In the remaining one half of respondents, 27.10 per cent move nearly 2 to 3 kilometers and 21.90 per cent pass through above 3 kilometers to reach the hospital.

HEALTH CARE SERVICE AND FACTOR DETERMINANTS OF HEALTH STATUS

It was found that most of the respondents say that doctor performance (86.20 percent), performance of nurse (88.60 percent), performance of lab technician (72.60 percent), medicine (86.20 per cent), fees structure (85.20 percent), operation theatre services (40.00 percent), space for outpatient (49.80 percent), fan facilities (73.80 percent), ambulance services (83.10 percent), overall opinion (55.40 percent) are good.

With regards majority of the respondents say that drinking water facilities (43.70 percent), space for inpatient (49.80 percent), bed facilities (42.50 percent) are moderate. Next of this, poor opinion of health care service were found in lab facilities (32.40 per cent), toilet facilities (50.80 per cent) and attendee's rest room (47 per cent). About 67.70 per cent reported that canteen facilities are not accessible in nature.

Among the household living environment variables medium standard of living index has a positive significance at 5 percent on health status. Next to this, high standard of living index has a positive significant influence at each 1 percent level on urban children health status. Children from those households which use good urban slums household facilities such as toilet, drinking water, sanitation facilities have positive impact on health status. The poor slums household's facility should be affected by children on various health problems like malaria, diarrea, skin and other problem.

From the regression analysis, it is summarized that the explanatory variables which positively influenced health status of children are age of children, child education, number of school going children, religion, social status, family income, family expenditure, father occupation, parental education type of school and standard of living index. Similarly variables which influence negatively are child education, social status, family size, father occupation and parental education.

SUGGESTIONS

The following suggestions are made based on the analysis and field observations:

- The government should take necessary steps to provide basic amenities such as treated drinking water sources, better sanitation facilities and infrastructure facilities as exist in the rest of the urban areas. It should be provided for both notified and non-notified slums through urban development schemes. It should be provided mainly to untenable slums also.
- To create awareness about the importance of education among slum children, particularly those who are drop out from school in middle of their studies. In addition to this, both the parents and children should be imparted about the need for higher education for better future and earnings.

- Awareness should be created among slum children about maintaining personal hygiene practices and possible preventive measures they can adopt in their homes which will prevent them from health hazards.
- Besides government, non-governmental organizations along with local community organizations should conduct proper campaigns and work for upliftment of slum children education and health status.

CONCLUSION

The present study has found that living environment was positively correlated with slum children health status. Open drainage system in most of the slums became water logged during the rains. Crowded living conditions along with stagnant and overflows of waste water around the living environment made children sick. However, insufficient space increased the risk of spread of infectious diseases such as respiratory infections, malaria, diarrhea, fever, etc. among children.

In few slums non-availability of public toilets made them to use open defecation in roadsides and nearby lands, which results in health problem with the children. Most of the slums have access to tap water from treated sources and few slum households have access to water from untreated sources for drinking purpose resulted in water borne diseases among children. In addition to this socio-economic background of households also influenced the health status of slum children. Thus high living environment slum households has positive effect on children health. Low level of living environment households children are suffering from various health problems.

This study has found that education of slum children associated with family size, monthly family income and other components of socio-economic status. Parents from poor economic background along with low education attainment did not impart the necessity of education among the slum children, which results in drop out. Parental education also influenced the level of education and type of school of children. Irregular attendance of children is mostly due to ill health, which is the result of living environment.

The gender inequality in level of education and type of school was evident from the study which demonstrated comparatively higher educational level for male than female children. Drop out was also higher in case of female children than male children. The implementation of various educational schemes like SSA and RMSA favoured slum children to get education at free of cost and availability of schools within reachable distance.

To conclude, mixtures of factors like poor basic amenities such as drainage, toilet, road, drinking water facilities, low literacy rate of parents, poverty, poor infrastructure and sanitary conditions could be reasons for the prevalence of diseases and low level of education among children in the current study. The prevalence of infectious diseases is prevalent among slum children in Salem District of Tamil Nadu. There is need to implement effective programmes providing support to slums for a multi-pronged approach focusing on redressing the failures and bringing formal system of basic amenities as exist in the rest of the town. Thus by providing basic amenities in slum, children health status can be improved in the study area.

BIBLIOGRAPHY

- African Population and Health Research Center (APHRC) (2002), **"Health and Livelihood Needs of Residents of Informal Settlements in Nairobi City, Nairobi"**, African Population & Health Research Center.
- Akhtar Hussain, Keramat Ali and Gunnar Kvale (1999), "**Determinants of Mortality among Children in the Urban Slums of Dhaka City, Bangladesh",** *Tropical Medicine and International Health,* 4 (11): 758–764.
- Alirol E. et al. (2011), "**Urbanisation and Infectious Diseases in A Globalised World**", *The Lancet,* 11(2):131-141.
- Alison M Buttenheim (2008), "**The Sanitation Environment in Urban Slums: Implications for Child Health",** *Population and Environment,* 30: 26–47.
- Amitabh Kundu (2013), "**Making Indian Cities Slum-Free: Vision and Operationalisation",** *Economic and Political Weekly,* 48(17):15-18.
- Banerji, M. (2009), "**Provision of Basic Services in the Slums and Resettlement Colonies Of Delhi",** Institute of Social Studies Trust.
- Becker (1965), "A Theory of the Allocation of Time", *The Economic Journal,* 75(299):493–517.
- Ben C. Arimah (2001), **"Slums as Expressions of Social Exclusion: Explaining the Prevalence of Slums in African Countries",** Paper Presented at United Nations Human Settlements Programme (UN-HABITAT), Nairobi, Kenya.
- Benjamin Stanwix (2009) **"Urban Slums in Gujarat and Rajasthan - Study of Basic Infrastructure in Seven Cities"** Mahila Housing SEWA Trust, Ahmedabad, India.
- Benta A Abuya, James Ciera and Elizabeth Kimani-Murage (2012) "Effect of Mother's Education on Child's Nutritional Status in the Slums of Nairobi" ***BMC Pediatrics,*** 12:80
- Brent Edelman and Arup Mitra (2007), **"Slums as Vote Banks and Residents. Access to Basic Amenities: The Role of Political Contact and its Determinants",** *Indian Journal of Human Development,* 1(1): 129-150.

- Census of India (2011), Town and Country Planning Organization, Metropolitan and Union Territories Division.
- Chandramouli, C (2003) "**Slums In Chennai: A Profile**" in Martin J. Bunch, V. Madha Suresh and T. Vasantha Kumaran, eds., Proceedings of the Third International Conference on Environment and Health, Chennai, India, 15-17, pp 82 – 88.
- Chandrasekhar S & Abhiroop Mukhopadhyay (2008), "**Multiple Dimensions of Urban Well-Being: Evidence from India**", Poverty, Gender & Youth, Working Paper No: 11, Population council, New York.
- Chandrasekhar S (2005) **"Growth of Slums, Availability of Infrastructure and Demographic Outcomes in Slums: Evidence from India**", Paper Presented During the Session on Urbanization in Developing Countries at the Population Association of America, Annual Meeting, Philadelphia, USA.
- **Chandrasekhar, S. (2005) "Growth of Slums, Availability of Infrastructure and Demographic Outcomes in Slums: Evidence from India",** Urbanization in Developing Countries at the Population Association of America, Philadelphia
- Charles Epari (2007) **"Enrolment And Gender Parity After Free Primary Education In Kenya: Looks Like Pro-Poor Private Schools In Nairobi's Slums Have A Point To Make",** African Population and Health Research Center (APHRC) Union for African Population Studies, Fifth African Population Conference, Arusha, Tanzania:10-14 December 2007.
- Chitnis Suma and Suvannathat C (1984), "**Schooling for Children of the Urban Poor",** In: P.J. Richards and Thomson, A.M. (eds.): Basic needs and the urban poor – An ILO-WEP study, London: Croom Helm.
- Claus C Portnery Yu-hsuan Suz (2012), "**Does Mother's Schooling Improve Child Health in Slums? Evidence from India**"
- D.C.V. Prasada Rao (1972), **"A Study of Social Aspects of Child Health in The Slum Communities of Pondicherry",** *The Indian Journal of Pediatrics*, 39(10): 311-316.
- Davis, Mike (2006), "**Planet of Slums",** Verso.
- Deepak Mili (2011) "**Migration and Healthcare: Access to Healthcare Services by Migrants Settled in Shivaji Nagar Slum of Mumbai, India"** *The Health,* 2(3): 82-85

- Erten Gokce (2009) "**Discrimination in Primary Education In The Slums Of Turkey: Problems About Equity Of Education**", *International Journal of Human and Social Sciences,* 4(2):96-101.
- Flood Joe (2006), "**Secure Tenure Survey Final Report**", Urban Growth Management Initiative.
- Frances Hunt (2008) "**Dropping Out from School: A Cross-Country Review of Literature**", *Research Monograph,* No: 16.
- Frederick Mugisha (2006) "**School Enrollment Among Urban Non-Slum, Slum and Rural Children In Kenya: Is The Urban Advantage Eroding?**", *International Journal of Educational Development,* 26: 471–482.
- Gabriel Gulis and Others (2004), "**Health Status of People of Slums in Nairobi, Kenya**", *Environmental Research,* 96: 219–227
- Geetha and Madhura Swaminathan (1996), "**Nutritional Status of Slum Children of Mumbai :A Socio-Economic Survey**", *Economic and Political Weekly,* 31(14):896-900.
- Ghosh S, Shah D (2004) "**Nutritional Problems in Urban Slum Children**" *Indian Pediatric,* 41(7): 682-696.
- Ghuncha Firdaus (2012), "**Urbanization, Emerging Slums And Increasing Health Problems: A Challenge Before The Nation: An Empirical Study With Reference To State Of Uttar Pradesh In India**", *Journal of Environmental Research and Management,* 3(9):0146-0152.
- Goswami Mihir, Kedia Geeta (2010), "**Socio-Demographic And Morbidity Profile Of Slum Area In Ahmedabad, India**", *National Journal of Community Medicine,*1(2):106-110.
- Govinda R,(1195), "**Status of Primary Education of the Urban Poor in India: An Analytical Review**", *Research Report* No. 105. UNESCO, Paris.
- Grace Bahalen Mundu and R B Bhagat (2008), "**Slum Conditions in Mumbai with Reference to the Access of Civic Amenities**", Published in IIPS Mumbai, ENVIS center, 5 (1)
- Grossman (1972a), "**The Demand for Health: A Theoretical and Empirical Investigation**", Occasional Paper-119, National Bureau of Economic Research, New York.
- Grossman (1972b), "**On the Concept of Health Capital and the Demand for Health**", *Journal of Political Economy,* 80(2):223–255.

- Guidelines for Rajiv Awas Yojana: Towards a Slum Free India by Ministry of Housing and Urban Poverty Alleviation, Government of India.
- Gyana Ranjan Panda and Trisha Agarwala (2013), "**Public Provisioning in Water and Sanitation: Study of Urban Slums in Delhi**", *Economic & Political Weekly*, 48(5):24-28.
- Haque MJ, Rashid M (2009), "**Nutritional Status of the Women of Reproductive Age with Some of Their Sociodemographic Characteristics of a Slum in Dhaka**", *Dinajpur Medical College Journal*, 2 (1): 2-7.
- Hatekar Neeraj and Rode Sanjay (2003), "**Truth about Hunger and Disease in Mumbai, Malnourishment among slum children**", *Economic and Political Weekly*, 38(43): 4604-4610.
- Hmwe Hmwe Kyu et al (2013) "Association of Urban Slum Residency with Infant Mortality and Child Stunting in Low and Middle Income Countries", Bio-Med Research International, Hindawi Publishing Corporation,pp1-12. http://dx.doi.org/10.1155/2013/604974
- International Institute of Population Sciences (IIPS) (2000), "**National Family Health Survey**" *(NFHS-2), 1998-99:* Mumbai, India.
- Jane A. Pryer, Stephen Rogers and Ataur Rahman (2006), "**Adult Illness in Dhaka Slum Households**", *Human Ecology Special Issue*, 14: 33-38
- Jane Pryer, Stephen Rogers, Ataur Rahman (2003) "**Work Disabling Illness as a Shock for Livelihoods and Poverty in Dhaka Slums, Bangladesh**", paper presented at the conference 'Staying Poor: Chronic Poverty and Development Policy' held at the University of Manchester, pp: 7 -9.
- Jurg Graf and Others (2008) "**Water Disinfection and Hygiene Behaviour in an Urban Slum in Kenya: Impact on Childhood Diarrhoea and Influence of Beliefs**", *International Journal of Environmental Health Research*, 18 (5):335–355.
- Karen Tatiana Montiel Lopez (2010) "**Financing Housing Improvements in Slum Communities in Ghana: The Case of the Kumasi Metropolis**", M.Sc Thesis submitted to the Department of Planning, Kwame Nkrumah University of Science and Technology, Kumasi.
- KarnS.K,ShigeoShikura and Harada Hideki(2003),Living Environment and Health of Urban poor: A study in Mumbai, Economic and Political Weekly, 38(34): 3575-3586.

- Kenkel (2000), "**Handbook of Health Economics**", *Elsevier, Amsterdam, 1(31): 1675–1720.*
- Kiranmai K, Saritha V, Mallika GP, Vara Lakshmi NR (2012), "**Assessment of Health Status of Women in Urban Slum**", *Indian Journal of Innovations Development,* 1(4):220-224.
- Kirti Ghei, Siddharth Agarwal, Malavika A. Subramanyam, S. V. Subramanian (2010), **"Association between Child Immunization and Availability of Health Infrastructure in Slums in India"** *Archives Of* Pediatrics *&* Adolescent Medicine,164(3): 243-249.
- Kumar, R., S. Kumar and Anurag (2007), **"Regional Dimension of Disparities in Slum Literacy in India"**, *Research and Practice in Social Sciences,* 2(2):103-123.
- Kundu N (2003), "**Urban Slum Reports: The Case of Kolkata, India"**, Nairobi: United Nations.
- Lee W Riley, Albert Ko, Alon Unger and Mitermayer G Reis (2007), **"Slum health: Diseases of neglected populations"**, *BMC International Health and Human Rights,* 7:2.
- M. Ali and L. Stevens (2009) "**Integrated Approaches to Promoting Sanitation: A Case Study of Faridpur, Bangladesh"** *Desalination,* 248(1-3): 1-7.
- M. S. Alamgir, M. A. Jabbar and M. S. Islam (2009) **"Assessing the Livelihood of Slum Dwellers in Dhaka City"**, *Journal of the Bangladesh Agricultural University,* 7(2): 373–380.
- Mandelker, D. R. (1969), **"Housing Codes, Building Demolition, and Just Compensation: A Rationale for the Exercise of Public Powers Over Slum Housing"**, *Michigan Law Review,* 67(4): **635-678**
- Md. Abdus Salam, Md. Abdul Alim, and Toshikuni Noguchi (2006) **"Spousal Abuse against Women and Its Consequences on Reproductive Health: A Study in the Urban Slums in Bangladesh"**, *Maternal and Child Health Journal,* 10(1):83-94.
- Md. Farid Uddin Khan (2010), **"Economic Consequences of Health Shocks and Coping Strategies: Evidence from Urban Poor Households in Bangladesh"**, Masters of Arts in Development Studies, International Institute of Social Studies, The Hague, The Netherlands, November, 2010
- Nalini Juneja (2000), **"Primary Education for All in the City of Mumbai, India: The Challenge Set by Local Actors"**, NIEPA, New Delhi.

- Nandita kapadia-kundu, Tara Kanitkar (2002), "**Primary Healthcare in Urban Slums**", *Economic and Political Weekly*, 21: 5086-8089.
- Naseeb Kumar Bhagat and Piyush Malaviya (2013), "Research Review on Socio-Environmental Status of Slum Dwellers", *Indian Journal of Applied Research*, 3(5):332-334.
- Naveen Kumar, Suresh Chand Aggarwal (2003), "**Patterns of Consumption and Poverty in Delhi Slums**", *Economic and Political Weekly*, 38(50):5294-5300.
- Neeraj M Srivastava, Shally Awasthi and Girdhar G Agarwal (2009), "**Care-Seeking Behavior and Out-Of-Pocket Expenditure for Sick Newborns among Urban Poor in Lucknow, Northern India: A Prospective Follow-Up Study**", *BMC Health Services Research*, 9:61.
- Netsayi N. Mudege et al (2008), "**How Insecurity Impacts on School Attendance and School Dropout among Urban Slum Children in Nairobi**", *International Journal of Conflict and Violence*, 2 (1) : 98–112.
- Nidhi Kotwal, Neelima Gupta and Shashi Manhas (2008), "**Impact of Work and Environment on Women Living in Urban Slums of Jammu City**", *Studies on Home and Community Science*, 2(2): 93-97.
- Nihar Ranjan Rout (2008), "**Slum Growth in Bhubaneswar: A Problem or Solution?**" *Institute of Town Planners, India Journal*, 5 (4): 59 – 64.
- Owoeye, J.O and Omole, F.K (2012), "**Built Environment Decay and Health Situation of Slum Dwellers in Residential Cores of Akure, Nigeria**", *American Journal of Human Ecology*, 1(2): 33-39.
- P. Panda, A.I. Benjamin and P. Zachariah (1993), "**Health Status of Under-Fives in a Ludhiana Slum**", *Health and Population - Perspectives and Issues*, 16(3&4):133-141.
- P.K. Mony, and Others (2006), "**Demography, Environmental Status and Maternal Health Care in Slums of Vellore Town, Southern India**", *Indian Journal of Community Medicine*, 31(4):230-233.
- Paramita Sengupta, Nina Philip and A. I. Benjamín (2010), "**Epidemiological Correlates of Under-Nutrition in Under-5 Years Children in an Urban Slum of Ludhiana**", *Health and Population: Perspectives and Issues*, 33 (1): 1-9
- Piyush Malaviya and Naseeb Kumar Bhagat (2013), "Urban Poverty and Health Risk Factors: A Case Study of Slum Dwellers of Jammu (J&K) India", *International Journal of Development and Sustainability*, 2(3):

- Prem Kumar (2010), "**Declining Number of Slums: Nature of Urban Growth",** *Economic and Political Weekly,*14(41):75-77.
- Punwani, Jyoti (Jan 10, 2011). **"Malnutrition Kills 56,000 Children Annually In Urban Slums",** The Times of India.
- Rajiv Sarkar and Others (2013), "**Burden of childhood diseases and malnutrition in a semi-urban slum in Southern India"**, *BMC Public Health,* 13:87.
- Rajnish Kumar, Satendra Kumar and Arup Mitra (2009), "**Social and Economic Inequalities: Contemporary Significance of Caste in India",** *Economic & Political Weekly,* 24(50):55-63.
- Ramamani Sundar and Abhilasha Sharma (2002), "Morbidity and Utilisation of Healthcare Services: A Survey of Urban Poor in Delhi and Chennai", *Economic and Political Weekly,* :4729- 4740
- Rashda Azhar, Sycda Khizra Aslam & Muhammad Akhtar (1992), **"The Living Conditions of Rural Migrants in City Slums",** *Pakistan Journal of Agricultural Sciences;* 29(1):37-39.
- Ratan Khasnabis, Tania Chatterjee (2007), "**Enrolling and Retaining Slum Children in Formal Schools: A Field Survey in Eastern Slums of Kolkata",** *Economic and Political Weekly,* 42(22): 2091-2098.
- Ronak B Patel and Others (2013), "**The High Cost Of Diarrhoeal Illness For Urban Slum Households-A Cost Recovery Approach: A Cohort Study",** *British Medical Journal Open,* 3(4).
- Sathya Sai Baba (2010), **"Slum Dog Millionaire-India's Real "Slum Dogs" Dream of a Better Life"** Wordpress.com
- Sean Fox (2008) "**On the Origins and Consequences of Slums",** CSAE (Centre for the Study of African Economies) Conference, Economic Development in Africa.
- Seetharamu A S (1998), "**Indian Mega Cities and Primary Education of the Poor: The Case of Bangalore City",** Paper presented at NIEPA at the Workshop on "Indian Mega Cities and Primary Education of the Poor".
- Sheikh Kabir Uddin Haider (2010) "**Factors of Migration on Urban Bangladesh: An Empirical Study of Poor Migrants in Rajshahi City**", *Pakistan Journal of Social Sciences (PJSS),* 30(2): 307-323.

- Sohail Ahmad, Mack Joong Choi (2011) "**The Context of Uncontrolled Urban Settlements in Delhi**" *The German Journal of Contemporary Asia*, 118: 75-90.
- Stuart Cameron (2009) **"Education in slums of Dhaka, Bangladesh"** Paper prepared for the 10th UKFIET International Conference on Education and Development.
- Stuart Cameron (2010) "**Access to and Exclusion from Primary Education in Slums of Dhaka, Bangladesh",** Create Pathways to Access, Research Monograph, No:45.
- Subhash Kumar (2012), "**An Economic Analysis of Environmental and Health Conditions of Urban Dweller Slums in Vizag"**, *International Journal of Social Science Tomorrow*, 1(10):1-13.
- Sufaira.C (2013), **"Socio Economic Conditions of Urban Slum Dwellers in Kannur Municipality**", IOSR Journal of Humanities and Social Science (IOSR-JHSS), 10(5):12-24.
- Sundari, S (2003) "**Quality of Life of Migrant Households in Urban Slums**" in Martin J. Bunch, V. Madha Suresh and T. Vasantha Kumaran, eds., Proceedings of the Third International Conference on Environment and Health, Chennai, India, 15-17.
- Sunil Kumar Karn, Shigeo Shikura and Hideki Harada (2003), **"Living Environment and Health of Urban Poor: A Study in Mumbai",** *Economic and Political Weekly*, :3575- 3586.
- Sunita Chugh (2011) **"Dropout in Secondary Education: A Study of Children Living in Slums of Delhi",** National University of Educational Planning and Administration (NUEPA), Occasional Paper No:37.
- The Hindu, March 01, 2009, Sunday.
- United Nations (2008), "**Integrated Water Sanitation and Waste Management in Kibera"**
- Upinder Sawhney (2013), "**Slum Population In India: Extent And Policy Response**" *International Journal of Research in Business and Social Science*, 2 (1): 47-56.
- Uttara Chauhan and Niraj Lal (1999), **"Public-Private Partnerships for Urban Poor in Ahmedabad : A Slum Project",** *Economic & Political Weekly*, 34(10/11) :636-642.

- Valerie A. Lewis (2009), **"Slums and Children's Disadvantage: The Case of India"** Ph.D., Dissertation, Princeton University, 189 pages.
- Valerie Lewis (2010), "**The Urban (Dis)Advantage: Slums, School and Children's Work**" paper presented at Population Association of America, Annual Meeting Program, Dallas, Texas, April15-17 2010, Hyatt Regency.
- Victoria Ijeoma Ononugbo, Akpan Ibanga Akpan, G. Solomon Osho (2010), **"An Empirical Analysis and Assessment of Housing Needs for the Low-Income People of Enugu Metropolitan Areas of Nigeria: Evidence from Statistical Housing Model Approach"**, *European Journal of Social Sciences,* 13(2): 243-270.
- Wendy Olsen and Others (2010), **"The Experience of Slum Dwellers in Chennai under the Economic and Environmental Insults of 2008-09"**, paper presented at the Conference 'The Hidden Contribution of Older People: Rethinking Age Poverty Oppoprtunity and Livelihoods', Centre for Law, Policy and Human Rights Studies and the Department of Humanities and Social Sciences, IIT, 19th and 20th March, Chennai.
- World Health Organization (2004), Water, Sanitation and Hygiene Links to Health: Facts and Figures.
- Y.P.Aggarwal , Sunita Chugh (2003), **"Learning Achievement of Slum Children in Government Schools of Delhi"**, National Institute of Educational Planning and Administration (NIEPA) Occasional Paper.
- Yuko Tsujita (2009) **"Deprivation of education in urban areas: A basic profile of slum children in Delhi, India"**, *IDE discussion paper,* No:199.
- Zakir Husian (2005) "**Analysing Demand for Primary Education: Muslim Slum Dwellers of Kolkata**" *Economic and Political Weekly,* 40(2):137-147.
- Zweifel and Breyer (1997), **"Health Economics"**, Oxford University Press, New York.